PRAISE FOR BORN LIBERAL, RAISED RIGHT

"I deeply respect Reb Bradley as one who has been gifted by God, particularly when it comes to truths that pertain to the family unit. It is my prayer that this book will be used to strengthen you, and to deepen your commitment to both God and family."

—Ray Comfort, best-selling author and co-host with Kirk Cameron of *The Way of the Master* television show

"This important book provides the foundation for understanding the cause of our country's problems, including the financial crisis of 2008."

—Alaska State Senator Joseph Orsini, Ph.D.

"I have known Reb Bradley for years and have always been amazed by his astute analysis of culture and human behavior. He has a rare gift of wisdom and a knack for communicating complex concepts in simple-to-understand terms. I have served in many levels of politics, both state and national, and I have found few as insightful as Reb. This book is sure to be a classic."

—Barbara Alby, California State Legislator, 1993-1998

"I have listened to Reb Bradley's CDs and read his books for years, and mine was one of many homes transformed by his message. Of all the voices speaking on family issues today, Reb's is the one that needs to be listened to most."

—Mario Rodriguez, California Commission on Peace Officer Standards, retired

"If you are trying to make sense of the current volatile political scene, then Reb Bradley's book is a must-read. Well-known in the evangelical Christian community for his books about parenting, marriage, and homeschooling, in these pages Reb examines politically correct child rearing and modern political philosophies, and, with clarity, shows how they have contributed to our current cultural decline and will negatively impact future generations.

Timely and challenging, Reb takes the reader into the depths of American socio-political trends. I was captivated as Reb unraveled, thread-by-thread, why our culture is in such decline. He doesn't just clarify this disturbing trend and leave us there—he also outlines how parents and government can make changes and reverse course."

—Frank R. Stephens is government and legislative affairs director for the Air Conditioning Trade Association of California at the state capital. He is a nationally published writer on politics, the environment, and religion.

"We at Rhino Technologies have followed Reb Bradley's speaking for several years through our recording work at conventions. It is clear that he has touched and helped literally THOUSANDS of families with his messages of encouragement, openness, honesty, and grace. With his gift of writing and speaking, he has been able to put into words what so many in our culture feel today about making a difference with their own families. Reb tells it straight, and we know the impact, because we have talked to thousands of those who have purchased his CDs and tapes, and taken to heart his messages."

—Mark Reinhardt, executive director of Rhino Technologies

"I've seen families significantly transformed by following Reb Bradley's practical approach to parenting. If you want to reclaim peace in your home— or even experience it for the first time—get your hands on his materials. It's not too late to change your relationship with your children—and make them the leaders of tomorrow that our country so desperately needs!"

—Nanette Woitas Holt, president of Image Ink publishing

"*Reb Bradley brilliantly takes us out of what C.S. Lewis called our slavery to the immediate past and gives the whole nation the long-term strategy of victory of good over evil, free enterprise over socialism, and all the other urgent battles we face. Whoever trains the children of the coming generation, controls the future. If we are ready to listen,* Born Liberal, Raised Right *can be our blueprint to save our nation's future.*"

—Dr. Marshall Foster, founder and president of the Mayflower Institute

BORN LIBERAL
RAISED RIGHT

BORN LIBERAL
RAISED RIGHT

HOW TO RESCUE AMERICA FROM MORAL DECLINE
—ONE FAMILY AT A TIME

By Reb Bradley

WND

BORN LIBERAL, RAISED RIGHT: How to Rescue America from Moral Decline—One
Family at a Time

A WND Books book
Published by WorldNetDaily
Los Angeles, CA

Jacket design by Linda Daly

WND Books are distributed to the trade by:

Midpoint Trade Books
27 West 20th Street, Suite 1102
New York, NY 10011

WND Books are available at special discounts for bulk purchases. WND Books, Inc.
also publishes books in electronic formats. For more information call (310) 961-4170 or
visit www.wndbooks.com.

First Edition

ISBN 10-Digit: 1935071009
ISBN 13-Digit: 9781935071006
E-Book ISBN 13-Digit: 9781935071587
E-Book ISBN 10-Digit: 1-935071-58-0

LCCN: 2008936370

Printed in the United States of America

10 9 8 7 6 5 4 3 2 1

Dedicated with love to my wife Beverly,
for believing in me.

TABLE OF CONTENTS

INTRODUCTION _____ xiii

Chapter One: *Adults Are Grown-Up Kids* _____ 1

Chapter Two: *A Healthy Society* _____ 9

Chapter Three: *We Are All Born Liberal* _____ 19

Chapter Four: *Raising Good Citizens* _____ 29

Chapter Five: *Governing with the* Heart, *Not the* Head _____ 47

Chapter Six: *Freedom to Be Enslaved* _____ 53

Chapter Seven: *Counterproductive Love* _____ 65

Chapter Eight: *Rescuing Victims* _____ 83

Chapter Nine: *Defensive Parenting* _____ 109

Chapter Ten: *Rewarding Bad Behavior* _____ 127

CONCLUSION _____ 137
APPENDICES _____ 141

THIS IS NOT ANOTHER BOOK ON PARENTING. It is not even primarily for parents. It is a book for those from all areas of the political spectrum concerned about current social trends and political philosophies, and who desire to understand the role parents play in shaping them. Those who would like a guide for rearing children can find practical help in my parenting seminar or in my book *Child Training Tips*.

I have written this book to answer questions asked by hundreds of thousands of people across the country: *What has happened to America in the last fifty years? Where did we go wrong? Why do so many children raised in good homes grow up with values so different from their parents? Who is responsible for America's moral downturn—the schools, the entertainment industry, the media? Is our problem rooted in poverty, racism, and a lack of good education; or are insensitivity, intolerance, and oppressive religion the real culprits?* The answers, you will discover, are not difficult to deduce. I anticipate that many will gain new insights into modern politics by what they read, but I expect that most will feel I am merely putting into words what they have felt all along. If, at the least, I can help people sharpen their thoughts, I will be satisfied.

The basic ideas in this book came to me in 1998. When I shared them with my friend Joseph Farah, he encouraged me to write a book, so the long journey began. I spent the next eight years collecting news reports, analyzing political philosophies, and formulating my thoughts. I am a slow and deliberate writer, so for the last year the task of writing has been more than arduous.

I have published portions of this work in two separate commentaries on *WorldNetDaily.com*. Part of Chapter One was originally published as "'What's happened to America?' The ultimate answer."[1] You will find a few random sentences from that article in other parts of the book, as well. Chapter Ten was originally run on *WorldNetDaily.com* in a simpler version under the title "When bad parenting turns into border policy."[2]

Some might assume that since I am a speaker and writer on family life issues that I am someone who has done everything right, and therefore feel qualified to address this subject.

Don't I wish that were true.

I do feel capable to tackle this subject, but it is not because I have done it all perfectly; hence the subtitle of my first parenting book—"What I wish I knew when my children were young." My gift does not seem to be doing things right the first time—I am jealous of people like that. No, my gift is that of analysis and documentation—I make mistakes, then learn from my mistakes, and share the answers with others. It is because I understand human nature and have taken careful notes on my parenting foibles, as well as the parenting journeys of so many thousands, that I have a basis for evaluating the dynamics of family life, culture, and politics.

ACKNOWLEDGMENTS

I want to thank my wife Beverly for her patience as she held the family together while I played absentee husband/father so much of the last year. She not only shouldered more than her weight at home, but she spent many hours going over the manuscript and recommending edits. She is my perfect counterpart in so many ways.

I am especially thankful for my children, who, for the last year, went to bed too many times without our bedtime chats and prayers.

I thank the Lord for giving me parents who were able to lay the foundation of so many important life principles.

And a big thanks to Joseph Farah for believing in my message and encouraging me to write the book.

A MERICA HAS A PROBLEM. The majority of parents, including conservatives, are raising their children to become liberals. Not on purpose, mind you—it's mostly by accident—but it is happening nonetheless.

"Oh," some might say, "that might be true for *moderates*, but that can't be so for *conservatives*! Why, every middle-aged Republican *I* know has watched his children grow up and join the Grand Ole Party."

Well, I certainly don't know enough about your personal life to dispute what you know of your friends, but I stick by my assertion—*American parents, conservatives included, are increasingly raising liberal children.*

By this I don't mean that increasing numbers of children are growing up to join liberal political parties—I mean that more and more young people arrive at adulthood with a liberal view of life. I think most of those over fifty would agree—our culture is far more liberal than it was five decades ago.

So how did that happen?

I have concluded that the responsibility lies primarily with parents. I propose that we, as grown-up children, are mostly products of our upbringing. It was our parents who, by their style of discipline and training, shaped our views of authority and developed our outlook on life. They may not have tried to train us to be of one political party or another, but we did develop our worldview as a result of their direct influence or the influences they allowed in our life; i.e., school, friends, television, etc. Either by their intent or neglect, by their action or inaction, we developed our views of justice, personal responsibility, care for the needy, freedom of expression, personal rights, etc. Without question, parents are responsible for creating each generation of adult citizens.

Chiefly, our response to parental influence is what produced any character that we have. And it is character, or lack of it, that produces our approach to government—whether we are voters or lawmakers. Politicians, for the most part, are nothing more than children who've grown up and attempt to govern using the same principles under which their parents raised them.

Let me reiterate. I am *not* saying that kids grow up and join the political parties of their parents because their parents intentionally set out to shape their political values. Not at all. I *am* saying that our worldviews are shaped in childhood by the way in which we are raised. The political biases of our college professors may certainly have helped us refine and codify our political philosophies, but our personal biases were already set when we arrived in college. Professors only had power to influence us because we leaned in their direction already. Our direction was set by our parents' style of leadership during our most impressionable years.

Still, some might question my assertion that every generation of adults is chiefly the product of those who raised them. One of the overall objectives of this book is to show how political perspectives are shaped by parents, but setting politics aside for the moment, consider just the present moral condition of our society as an example of the power of parental influence.

In the last few years, news reports have brought a heightened awareness of uniquely abhorrent crimes—unspeakable deeds committed by young people, seemingly without tinge of conscience. In reality, it is not just a perception we have received from news reports. Morality in America has, in fact, been declining for several decades. And it is parents who have the greatest responsibility.

CHAPTER ONE

ADULTS ARE GROWN-UP KIDS

"What's done to children, they will do to society."

—Dr. Karl Menninger[1]

O N JANUARY 29, 1979, sixteen-year-old Brenda Spencer opened fire with a .22-caliber rifle at Grover Cleveland Elementary School in San Diego, California. The principal and a custodian were left dead, and eight children and a police officer were wounded. Brenda later explained that she didn't like Mondays and just wanted to liven up the day. She said she had no reason for the killing spree and found it a lot of fun.[2]

Heartless murderers have existed for centuries, but modern, civilized America had never experienced such casual disregard for innocent life from one of its own "innocent" children. Unfortunately, this was not an isolated or fluke incident. It was the first public manifestation of a growing immorality in our culture, and the beginning of a trend.

> • *January 21, 1985*: Fourteen-year-old James Kearbey went to school and began shooting. He killed the principal and wounded three others.[3]

> • *September 26, 1988*: James Wilson went to a Greenwood, South Carolina elementary school and shot seven students and two teachers, leaving two eight-year-old girls dead.[4]

• *January 17, 1989*: Patrick Purdy opened fire with an AK-47 assault rifle on a playground at a Stockton, California elementary school. Five children died at his hands and twenty-nine others, along with a teacher, were wounded.[5]

• *May 1, 1992*: Armed with a shotgun and a sawed-off .22 rifle, Eric Houston returned to his former high school in Olivehurst, California. Angry about a failing grade he had received in civics class, he killed four people, wounded nine others, and took approximately eighty students hostage before surrendering.[6]

• *January 18, 1993*: Seventeen-year-old Scott Pennington was upset over a bad grade on his report card, so he brought a gun to East Carter High School in Grayson, Kentucky and killed his English teacher and a janitor, and then held twenty-two classmates hostage.[7]

Ten similar school incidents would take more innocent lives before April 20, 1999. On that day at Columbine High School, when fifteen people died and nearly twenty more were wounded, we thought it couldn't get any worse.[8] But fifteen school shootings later, on April 16, 2007, Virginia Tech lost thirty-two students and faculty to a heartless student killer.[9]

Heinous acts of casual disregard for life, unheard of fifty years ago, have become a familiar item on the evening news: students killing classmates, children murdering their playmates, teenaged mothers abandoning their newborn babies to die. One survey of prison inmates over sixty years old revealed an overwhelming consensus that the young criminals now entering prisons are of a new breed—one which lacks a conscience. What's happened to the youth in America?

Some postulate that senseless killings are a result of children being allowed to play with toy guns, or exposure to too much violent television, music, or video games. Others suggest that weak gun control laws are responsible. Still others think it is the absence of after-school programs. Societal trends, however, suggest that these gruesome crimes are merely symptomatic of a breakdown of moral fiber and an escalated crime rate.

Although the crime rate has dropped slightly since 1991, it remains near an all-time high. According to statistics compiled by the Federal Bureau of Investigation, since 1960 incidents of robbery have increased by 250 percent, rape is up by 318 percent, and the rate of aggravated assault has grown by 329 percent. Overall, violent crimes have tripled in the last fifty years.[10] What's happened to America?

While crime is increasing, stability of family relationships is on a downward spiral. On a national average, marriages are now dissolving at approximately a 40 percent rate of divorce.[11] The "generation gap" identified in the '60s has continued to widen. Now, adolescents are not only alienated from their parents, but they sue them for "emancipation." And, in more than a few cases, children born with birth defects have sued their parents for not aborting them. What's worse, the American masses are not shocked by such social disintegration; rather their love for sleaze talk shows reveals that they find it entertaining. What's happened to America?

Academically, student success is near an all-time low. Since 1963, SAT scores have dropped significantly, from an average score of 1081 in 1963[12] down to a score of 1017 more recently.[13] In public schools, where teachers a generation ago reported the greatest challenges to be "talking in class" and "chewing gum," now violence, drugs, and sexual assault top the list. The disciplined, orderly classroom, providing the optimum learning environment, is a thing of the past. Students no longer typically regard teachers with respect or honor, nor take as seriously the education teachers try to give. What's happened to America?

Sexually, we have become a nation ruled by its passions. In the last few decades, premarital and extramarital sexual activity has increased markedly. Graphic pornography, once available only on the black market, and popular only with the "lower elements of society," can now be found in corner video stores and reputable hotels, and is enjoyed as entertainment by the masses. In the 1950s, most teenage girls prized their chastity and were coached by people like Ann Landers to avoid "going steady" lest it lead to "going all the way."[14] In 2002, a study by the U.S. Center for Disease Control revealed that 47 percent of female teenagers had had sex.[15] This increase in premarital and extramarital sexual activity has produced a significant increase in STDs,[16] including the spread of the deadly AIDS virus.[17] Our forty-second president, who by virtue of his office was the nation's premier role model for children, received a high approval rating from the American people even after being exposed for his brazen lechery and deceit. What we once considered outrageous or perverse is now "normal" and even admirable. What's happened to America?

What is the cause of our society's condition? Are we in severe moral decline because of poverty? If so, will society be cured if everyone has money? Is it education? If so, will morality return if our schools do a better job? Is the problem entertainment? If so, will we reduce violence if we limit everyone's access to violent television, video games, and music? Is it a lack of after-school programs, which, if funded, will restore order to our world?

A society is not an entity in itself—with a collective mind—it is simply a reflection of the individuals that comprise it. Societies, therefore, do not fall—the individuals in them do. Consequently, the problem and its cure go back to the individuals in a society. To solve a society's moral problems, the individuals who comprise it must be cured. The simple truth is that the individuals who contribute to America's present moral decadence are lacking a specific virtue. They are deficit a certain character quality necessary to maintain a civilized society.

What has happened to the individuals in America is that they are by and large deficit the key ingredient of maturity—*self-control*. Any society that is out of control is comprised of individuals who lack self-control. We as a nation have moral problems today primarily because our individual members do not have the ability to adequately restrain themselves.

Can it be that simple? Yes. In modern America, most individuals are ruled by their passions—they lack self-restraint—they cannot say "no" to themselves. If they had the virtue of self-control, they and the society they comprise would not be so "out of control."

When they are angry, they give vent to their anger and lash out in violent actions or words. When they lust, they gobble up pornography like candy and pursue those they lust after, with no thought to wedding vows or little thought to risk. When they

4

covet, they steal to obtain or they cheat to achieve. When they need an escape from stress, they drink, inhale, or swallow a pill to numb the pain. When it's to their advantage, they have little regard for integrity, but lie, mislead, or break a promise. The addiction to personal gratification rules the individuals who comprise America. The land of the "free" has become inhabited by slaves.

A few decades ago people were just as human as we are in this decade. Like us, they got angry, they lusted, they coveted, and they drowned their grief by one means or another. But in one important way, they were different from us—they had greater self-control. Because they were more self-restraining, they did not allow themselves to be ruled by their anger; hence the murder rate was markedly less. They lusted, but they had greater sexual self-restraint, so had sexual contact with fewer people and contracted fewer STDs. They coveted other people's money and possessions, but they had the ability to not act on their covetousness; hence fewer were compelled to steal. In the last forty years we have lost the virtue of self-control. No longer is our society populated by individuals who can restrain or "govern" themselves. To lack the capacity to control one's urges or passions is to lack what our nation's Founders called personal "self-government."

When a society is comprised of individuals with self-control, fewer laws and regulations are needed, police have less to do, doors need not be locked, and lost items are routinely returned to the owners. In such a society, a man's word is his bond and a handshake solemnizes a promise. A society whose people are temperate is one that can remain free, but a society in which the people lack temperance is one that requires more laws and greater governmental controls.

Our Founding Fathers understood the passionate bent of human nature. They knew when they established our nation that, for a liberty-based government to succeed with minimal controls, it would require that the citizens each be self-governing.

For those who might not yet grasp what I am saying, I suggest that you check with a schoolteacher—they see this manifested every day in classrooms, which are microcosms of society. Students who have the most self-control require the least supervision—they can be trusted to do what is right whether someone is watching or not, and therefore can be entrusted with the most liberty. Such children can immediately stop talking when told to and are generally faithful to obey the rules. Sadly, too few students such as this exist today. Young teachers can only dream of what it was like to teach forty years ago, back when the biggest problems were students occasionally chewing gum and chatting in class. Struggle for classroom control has become a consuming chore since parents began sending children to school who disrespect authority and lack self-restraint.

Still do not get it? Then ask a police officer about the importance of self-control—they are forced to use their Taser guns on people every day who lack the capacity to simply close their mouths and immediately do what they are told. Daily in America, Tasers are needed to subdue uncooperative citizens, who could have passed up some pain and might even have avoided arrest if they had just shut their mouths and followed the officer's instructions. Certainly, many get tased because they are drunk or high, but plenty bring pain on themselves purely because they never learned from their parents how to close their lips and do what they were told.

Most who earn a tasing do not think they deserve it. They have grown up with an exalted view of their own importance, and so are merely exercising what they think is their right to express their feelings in protest of an unreasonable request by an authority figure. They feel compelled to say everything that is on their minds, and are literally incapable of submitting themselves to an authority greater than themselves. At the least, the kid who cannot stop himself from mouthing off to his parents or teachers is a candidate for a future tasing. A little time surfing the Internet will verify what I am saying—video Web sites abound with clips of arrests made of mouthy, out-of-control grown-ups.

The bottom line is that whether it is in a classroom, a community, or a nation, self-controlled people maintain order and make good citizens. People who never learned to control themselves or their passions do not.[18] It's really not that complicated.

Where has Self-Control Gone?

The question is not, *how did we as a society lose self-control*, but rather, *why do we as individuals fail to possess what our predecessors obviously had*? Self-control is not learned in school. It is not a byproduct of getting older. It is certainly not learned from childhood peers. Self-control is a deep-rooted character trait trained into children by their parents in the first few years of life. It was the observation of Thomas Jefferson that, *"the qualifications for self-government in society are not innate. They are the result of habit and long training."*[19]

The true cause of America's decline is that most modern parents were not raised to value self-control as a virtue, so few have trained their children to have it. They may have taught their children to respect the rainforest or to use condoms when their passions rule them, but they have not given them the virtue that they need most of all—that society needs most of all.

Fifty years ago, America was a more moral place—not because of government programs, not because of tighter gun controls, and not because schools were better funded. Our communities and schools were safer because parents raised their children with the ability to not act on their every whim.

A child who learns self-control does not habitually hit his brothers and sisters when he wants his way, and typically does not grow up to lie, cheat, steal, murder, or violate his wedding vows. He may feel like sassing his parents, his teachers, or his boss, but he is able to control himself and speak with respect. He may feel like making an obscene gesture at the driver who cut him off, but he is able to restrain himself and not escalate a conflict. He may feel like shooting his classmates, but he has the ability to *not* do it. He has passions and all the natural drives, but they do not rule him. Because his passions are not calling the shots in his life, he has discretion and is free to make wise decisions. Because his craving for pleasure does not rule him, he is faithful and reliable in duties. Because he is not a slave to self-gratification, he has less to cover up with lies.

Parents are with their children during the most influential years of their lives, and their position as parents gives them the opportunity to have the most monumental impact. But if parents elevate "self-expression" and "self-actualization," and if they confuse indulgence with love, they fail to teach their children the most basic character quality needed by each member of society.

The problem for most American parents is they themselves lack self-control—they cannot pass on what they do not have. Or if they have it, they do not know how they got it, so are unable to duplicate in their children what their own parents did in them.

Most parents are preoccupied with keeping their children happy, and inadvertently raise kids with an exalted view of their own importance. Such kids do not develop self-control, but remain full of the opposite—*self-indulgence*. They grow up to believe that it is their right to have their way in life, and will pursue their own personal happiness at the expense of others. Is that not the heart of an adult who is out of control? Is that not the perspective of a thief who thinks he is more important than the rightful owner of property, or the outlook of a murderer who violates another's right to life? At the least, is not such self-centeredness at the root of so many broken marriages?

I restate my premise—every generation of adults is the product of those who raised them. If a society is out of control, it is because its citizens were raised by parents who failed to give them self-control. If children who have been allowed to elevate self-gratification and who lack moral temperance grow up to vote or assume political office, should we not expect that their approach to government will reflect the bent of their outlook on life?

CHAPTER TWO

A HEALTHY SOCIETY

"The government...can never be in danger of degenerating into a monarchy, an oligarchy, an aristocracy, or any other despotic or oppressive form so long as there shall remain any virtue in the body of the people."

—George Washington[1]

WHY ARE SO MANY AMERICANS raising liberal children? Here's my hypothesis: All humans are born with the same predisposition toward life. We may each be born with our unique personalities, but we have the same bent—by nature we are all born *liberal*. I propose that liberalism is, in fact, the natural condition of the human heart. For us to grow into conservatives, we must be trained against our nature.

In this age of technology, one might say that liberalism is our "default" operating condition. Throughout our childhoods, our parents must work hard and change our settings to keep us from operating in our default mode. If parents are successful, we enter adulthood with our new settings fully locked in. Left untrained, all children would grow up liberal in their outlook.

Some might still wonder if I am suggesting that inadequate parenting by Republican parents is causing children to grow up and join the Democratic Party. Not necessarily. Children raised in Republican homes tend to remain Republican, and those reared in Democratic homes tend to remain Democratic. Researcher Arthur

Brooks of Syracuse University noted that 80 percent of citizens who express a political party preference vote like their parents.[2] I am saying that if conservative parents do not understand that conservatives are groomed by training children against their nature, they will be careless in their parenting and accidentally rear children to be liberal in their outlook. Such children may grow up and join the Republican Party. They may become adults and proudly wear the label "conservative." However, inwardly and philosophically, they will be more liberal than their parents. Hence, the Republican Party will continue to become increasingly liberal.

This should especially concern conservatives who have been sitting back smugly because they know that Republican families are steadily growing larger than those of Democrats. For three decades, some conservatives have found security in the fact that Republican families have 41 percent more children than Democrats and soon will outnumber them.[3] Conservatives must beware—just because liberals choose lap dogs over children, there is nothing to celebrate. Liberals will not need to outnumber conservatives. Given the present inability of conservatives to rear conservative children, all that liberals really need to do is sit back and wait. If they merely bide their time, the next generation of conservatives will be just as liberal as they are. It has been said that evil triumphs when good men do nothing. So also, for liberalism to succeed, parents need not do anything.

The problem is that many younger conservatives do not truly understand conservatism. They are attracted to the "no nonsense" attitude associated with conservative foreign policy. They embrace the logic of conservative ideas espoused by right-wing talk show hosts, but in their own personal lives they lack the moral anchor that defines the term "conservative." In fact, more and more, their lifestyles reveal that they embrace the moral values of liberals. They are, therefore, incapable of raising their children with the character that produces conservatism.

Before going any further, it's important to spell out the fundamental principles of human nature, the basics of proper parenting, and the moral differences between liberals and conservatives. Let me briefly summarize here some of the differences between liberals and conservatives. In Chapter Three, I will explain the root tendencies of human nature and in Chapter Four, the basics of effective parenting.

Distinctives of Liberals and Conservatives

Conservatives might create a caricature of liberals as big-spending, soft-on-crime, whiny pursuers of big government. On the other hand, liberals might characterize conservatives as heartless bigots who favor big business and oppress free speech and the needy. Caricatures aside, based strictly on the definition of the words, let us establish the differences between *liberal* and *conservative*.

Before I define my terms, let me say up front that my definitions will not accurately describe every individual who identifies him or herself as *conservative* or *liberal*. That is for a couple of reasons. First, there are few truly pure liberals or conservatives—most liberals have some conservative traits and many conservatives have some liberal traits. Second, few people actually understand the rudimentary elements that form the basis for their label. That, in fact, is one of the reasons I have written this book. If, as you read, you struggle with my definitions, then I want to encourage you to have an open mind—this book may change your life.

Defining Terms

I researched more than a dozen dictionaries, and I believe it is accurate to say that to be politically *liberal* is to be freed from restraints, liberated from moorings; ever-changing, having an evolving basis for values, not bound by tradition or orthodoxy. In American politics, this means that pure liberals have an expanding view of the Constitution—a "living document" they call it—that should not be bound by the intent of its Framers. And because liberals have a progressive view of morals, they feel free to abandon the restrictive moral values prominently held by society at the time our nation was founded. Such liberation from outdated values, in fact, they view as merely an appropriation of the "freedom of expression" guaranteed by the Constitution.

A key tenet of liberalism is what liberals call "compassionate government." They identify themselves as the champions of compassion. They profess special concern for the poor and oppressed. They strive to be guardian of the rights of those they perceive to be the downtrodden. Consequently, they want to guarantee entitlements for the disadvantaged, create housing and healthcare for the homeless, provide special care for children and grandchildren of those who historically suffered discrimination, secure protection for those hurt or offended by denigrating language, and grant special rights to victims of potential discrimination or abuse. They feel especially strong about protecting personal rights, particularly the right to unrestricted "self-expression." All of this compassion and help can best be realized, they believe, through laws, judicial decisions, and properly administered government programs.

To be *conservative* means to be anchored by an unchangeable foundation; making present decisions on the basis of previously established absolutes, therefore, progressing with care and restraint. In American politics this means that conservatives not only accept, but submit themselves to the Constitution as a moral and civil anchor. They attempt to hold strictly to the Framers' intents, because they view them as individuals who had an astute, if not superior, grasp on the core principles of justice, liberty, and self-government.

Contrary to the caricature of conservatives as people only concerned about big business and personal wealth, a principal element of true conservatism is *compassion*. However, unlike the liberal approach to social problems, true conservatives seek to help people achieve success through emphasizing *personal responsibility* — a key tenet of conservatism. They will not unreservedly provide money or housing for the disadvantaged lest laziness, dependence, and an ungrateful outlook be cultivated. Instead, they will insist a capable person take responsibility for himself and labor for his own keep. Conservatives believe America's greatness is rooted in the strength of character of each of its citizens. They, therefore, emphasize the individual's need for self-government, self-reliance, and personal fortitude, which they believe makes it possible to limit the size and scope of government—a critical trait for a free society.

A Healthy Society

Conservatives and liberals share the belief that government's job is to protect society from harmful influences. They disagree sharply, however, on what is harmful. A *liberal* believes strongly in the right to "free expression," meaning the liberty to speak one's mind and pursue personal pleasure, so long as no harm comes to others. Consequently, the liberal considers any threat to censor those expressions or restrain those liberties as harmful to society and will fight vehemently to protect them. A *conservative* also believes strongly in freedom of expression, but views pursuing passion without restraint as a character deficiency that is morally harmful to society. Both camps want society's good, but they strongly disagree on how to define what is good.

Consider, for example, that many *liberals* believe government has a duty to give away condoms and fund AIDS research, because citizens should have freedom to pursue sexual passions without suffering fatal consequences. They stress that abortions must be legal, so that people can engage in sexual activity without risk of bringing a child into the world when *recreation*, not *procreation*, is their goal. It is the duty of our tax-funded government, they insist, to secure these protections.

Likewise, a *conservative* embraces the First Amendment's protection of free expression, and boldly defends the right to "life, liberty, and the pursuit of happiness." However, he believes that freedom to pursue personal passions without restraint is neither prudent, nor morally responsible for individuals, and, therefore, damages society's moral fiber. He is convinced that high crime rates and moral disintegration characterize any society populated by individuals ruled by their passions. Conservatives share the view of the Founding Fathers that true liberty in society is only possible when individuals are self-governing; that is, they have the capacity to not act out on their hedonistic and base desires. Consequently, conservatives emphasize personal moral restraint, while liberals passionately pursue laws that secure moral license. To the conservative, liberty is only possible when individuals are free *from*. To the liberal, liberty means being free *to*. Hence, liberals and conservatives have significantly conflicting views of government.

As I stated earlier in this chapter, among both liberals and conservatives, there are some who will take issue with my definitions. They proudly wear the label "conservative" or "liberal," but they feel my description of their preferred philosophical association is too simplistic or effectively excludes them. They may even feel I have aligned them with their opponents. If that is you, then I want to encourage you that there are good things ahead. What distresses you now, you may find benefits you later.

What Makes for a Healthy Society?

When our Founding Fathers established our nation, they sought to create a society greater than any other—not for their own glory, but for the sake of generations to come. They had experienced living under the oppression of theocratic monarchies, and desired to create a free society in which all men were guaranteed the right to oversee their own lives, enjoy personal liberty, and pursue happiness. To safeguard these rights, this new government would be administered not by a sovereign monarch, but by the people themselves, deriving its "powers from the consent of the governed."[4] To conceive of such a radical and noble idea took men of extraordinary vision. To design such a masterful plan for our constitutional republic, replete with checks and balances, took men of superior intellect and wisdom. These statesmen pledged their lives, their fortunes, and their sacred honor to generations of strangers yet unborn, and demonstrated a depth of character found in few modern politicians.

The architects of our nation were men who understood the value of virtue and personal integrity. They knew that for this experiment in national self-government to succeed, it would require that each of America's citizens place a high value on individual self-government. Samuel Adams, in a letter to John Adams on October 4, 1790, said that people must learn *"...the art of self government without which they never can act a wise part in the government of societies."*[5] James Madison, known as the "Father of our Constitution," emphasized the importance of personal moral restraint when he declared, *"We have staked the whole of all our*

14

political institutions upon the capacity of mankind for self-government, upon the capacity of each and all of us to govern ourselves, to control ourselves. ..."[6]

The Founders knew that to limit the need for far-reaching governmental controls and to preserve individuals' freedom, American society would need to emphasize morality and virtue. Since America was to be a nation of people who would rule themselves, the preservation of moral fiber was imperative. Consider the following statements made by our Founders:

> *"Only a virtuous people are capable of freedom. As nations become corrupt and vicious, they have more need of masters."* Benjamin Franklin, Signer of the Declaration of Independence and the Constitution[7]

> *"It is certainly true that a popular government cannot flourish without virtue in the people."* Richard Henry Lee, Signer of the Declaration of Independence[8]

> *"The only foundation for a useful education in a republic is to be laid in religion. Without this there can be no virtue, and without virtue there can be no liberty, and liberty is the object and life of all republican governments."* Benjamin Rush, Signer of the Declaration of Independence[9]

> *"The government...can never be in danger of degenerating into a monarchy, an oligarchy, an aristocracy, or any other despotic or oppressive form so long as there shall remain any virtue in the body of the people."* George Washington[10]

> *"Neither the wisest constitution nor the wisest laws will secure the liberty and happiness of a people whose manners are universally corrupt."* Samuel Adams, Signer of the Declaration of Independence[11]

> *"Give up money, give up fame, give up science, give the earth itself and all it contains rather than do an immoral act. And never suppose that in any possible situation, or under any circumstances, it is best for you to do a dishonorable thing, however slightly so it may appear to you. Whenever you are to do a thing, though it can never be known but to yourself, ask yourself how you would act were all the world looking at you, and act accordingly. Encourage*

all your virtuous dispositions, and exercise them whenever an opportunity arises, being assured that they will gain strength by exercise, as a limb of the body does, and that exercise will make them habitual. From the practice of the purest virtue, you may be assured you will derive the most sublime comforts in every moment of life, and in the moment of death." Thomas Jefferson, Signer of the Declaration of Independence[12]

"Our liberty depends on our education, our laws, and habits...it is founded on morals and religion, whose authority reigns in the heart, and on the influence all these produce on public opinion before that opinion governs rulers." Fisher Ames, Framer of the First Amendment[13]

"Without morals a republic cannot subsist any length of time; they therefore who are decrying the Christian religion, whose morality is so sublime & pure, [and] which denounces against the wicked eternal misery, and [which] insured to the good eternal happiness, are undermining the solid foundation of morals, the best security for the duration of free governments." Charles Carroll, Signer of the Declaration of Independence[14]

"[W]e have no government armed with power capable of contending with human passions unbridled by morality and religion...Our constitution was made only for a moral and religious people. It is wholly inadequate to the government of any other." John Adams, Second president of the United States[15]

"[I]t is religion and morality alone which can establish the principles upon which freedom can securely stand. The only foundation of a free constitution is pure virtue." John Adams[16]

"Of all the dispositions and habits which lead to political prosperity, religion and morality are indispensable supports. In vain would that man claim the tribute of patriotism who should labor to subvert these great pillars of human happiness, these firmest props of the duties of man and citizens. The mere politician, equally with the pious man, ought to respect and to cherish them. A volume could not trace all their connexions with private and public felicity. Let it simply be asked, Where is the security for property, for reputation, for life, if the sense of religious obligation desert the oaths, which are the instruments of investigation in Courts of Justice?

> *"And let us with caution indulge the supposition that morality can be maintained without religion. Whatever may be conceded to the influence of refined education on minds of peculiar structure, reason and experience both forbid us to expect that national morality can prevail in exclusion of religious principle. It is substantially true, that virtue or morality is a necessary spring of popular government. The rule, indeed, extends with more or less force to every species of free government. Who, that is a sincere friend to it, can look with indifference upon attempts to shake the foundation of the fabric?"* George Washington[17]

Finally, consider these words of Thomas Jefferson:

> No government can continue good but under the control of the people; and people so demoralized[18] [lacking good morals] and depraved[19] as to be incapable of exercising a wholesome control, their reformation must be taken up ab incunabulis.[20] Their minds [must] be informed by education what is right and what wrong, be encouraged in habits of virtue and deterred from those of vice by the dread of punishments, proportioned indeed, but irremissible.[21] In all cases, follow truth as the only safe guide and eschew error which bewilders us in one false consequence after another in endless succession. These are the inculcations[22] necessary to render the people a sure basis for the structure of order and good government.[23]

In case you missed what Jefferson was trying to communicate, it was his opinion that by nature, people are depraved, immoral, and lacking self-control. He therefore believed that the only way that the American style of government could be maintained was to instruct everyone in right and wrong from birth, and train them toward good habits and virtue through disciplinary consequences. Political self-government, he said, requires that citizens be raised to despise dishonesty and embrace personal integrity through instruction and repeated admonitions. His perspective was representative of the majority of our Founding Fathers.

Our Founders certainly understood that the character of a society is determined by the character of the individuals in it. When a society fails to foster the virtues of integrity and personal responsibility, it will slide into moral decline.

The late British social anthropologist Joseph Daniel Unwin, famous for his study of world civilizations, discovered that a society ruled by its passions loses the moral fiber necessary to maintain civility. Studying the decline and fall of eighty world empires, Unwin determined that the loss of self-restraint, culminating in unlimited sexual expression, precipitated each empire's demise.[24] Either the individuals in those societies became personally ruled by their passions, resulting in lawlessness and social chaos, or in their hedonism they lost the moral fiber necessary to successfully protect themselves militarily. America on both fronts has great reason for concern. The obvious question becomes, what must we do to change course and reverse our present moral decline?

The increasing social problems in our country are not caused by poor education, poverty, inadequate after-school programs, or lax gun laws. Our problems have increased as parents have lost sight of how to raise children. We must cure the problem and not continue to waste our tax dollars treating the symptoms. To offer a new government program in response to social ills is like a doctor treating a cancerous tumor with Novocain and a Band-Aid. Our nation's problems have arisen just as our Founders warned they would. They stem from a common lack of character and decline in personal morality. If we are to see our nation change, we must help the next generation of parents embrace good character and learn how to pass it on to their children.

CHAPTER THREE

WE ARE ALL BORN LIBERAL

"To understand…principles of human behavior…we must first begin by accepting the basic premise that all humans are born hedonists (aka narcissists) and have an intrinsic need to seek pleasure, avoid pain, and engage in those activities that best accomplish both with the least amount of effort."

—Dr. Terry G. Shaw[1]

I F IN FACT, TO HAVE A SOCIETY OF VIRTUE and high morals requires that parents know how to raise children with good character, the rearing of such children will require the right foundation. Parents must understand the natural bent of the human heart, they must know what good character is, and they must have a realistic plan to train their children toward this character. Without that foundation, parents will be helpless to slow our nation's present descent into moral decadence. In fact, they will likely contribute to its continued demise. My hope and prayer is that parents and the politically minded will catch a vision of all that I share here.

The Core of Liberalism in Human Nature

In the beginning of Chapter Two I declared that liberalism is the natural condition of the human heart from birth. This idea first struck me back in 1998. I was listening to a radio talk show host list the traits of liberals. As the author of a book on parenting, I was amazed at what I heard—the traits he ascribed to liberal politicians were the exact same traits of indulged children and indulgent parents I had documented in my parenting book. The more I thought about it, the more it became clear that liberals may be *shaped* by liberal influences in schools, the media, and entertainment, but they are not *created* by them. Liberalism is inherent to the passionate bent of human nature. Liberals are merely inadequately trained children who grew up and now lead using principles they gleaned from their upbringing.

To be born liberal means that we are all born emotional, passionate beings. We come into the world determined to survive and we vehemently express ourselves to get what we need: "Waaa!" and Momma feeds us; "Waaa!" and our diaper is changed; "Waaa!" and we are put down for a nap. As infants, our strong will can keep us comfortable and alive—the more outspoken we are, the more our needs are met. However, as we start to grow, we no longer cry only for necessities—we crave pleasure, too. At nine months old, if it's Uncle Bert's watch we want, we grab on and scream when he does not give it to us. Uncle Bert might laugh and marvel at our strength, but he easily pulls his watch away, sparking our anger. We are so furious that if we were seven feet tall and coordinated, Uncle Bert would be dead, and we would have his watch. The will-to-survive that kept us alive as newborns is revealed as a will-to-be-gratified as we grow older.

A grasp of liberal as well as conservative outlooks requires that we understand the self-centered drive of human nature. From birth we are all driven by *passion*—we want what we want, when we want it, and we refuse things we do not want. Hence, as young children we beg or scream for ice cream, and turn our noses up at Brussels sprouts. By nature we hate having to wait and demand immediate gratification—we throw fits when we do not get our way. From our first year of life we want to gratify ourselves, and loathe the idea of reaping consequences for our actions. It is our parents' job to train us to have self-control—to teach us that we can find contentment and security in life without fulfilling all our passions. They must work diligently to teach us that we do not need to be ruled by our will-to-be-gratified.

We Are All Born Liberal

In 1926, Governor Theodore Christianson of Minnesota established the Minnesota Crime Commission to study crime and evaluate its causes. At the end of its research the commission concluded that criminal tendencies were not a result of poverty, education, or environment. Instead, it offered the following observation:

> Every baby starts life as a little savage. He is completely selfish and self-centered. He wants what he wants when he wants it: his bottle, his mother's attention, his playmate's toys, his uncle's watch, or whatever. Deny him these and he seethes with rage and aggressiveness which would be murderous were he not so helpless. He's dirty; he has no morals, no knowledge, no developed skills. This means that all children, not just certain children but all children, are born delinquent. If permitted to continue in their self-centered world of infancy, given free rein to their impulsive actions to satisfy each want, every child would grow up a criminal, a thief, a killer, a rapist.[2]

This commission, studying American culture that had not yet sunk to our present level, concluded that the potential for crime and social failure was in each one of us at birth. The clear message was that society's future is in the hands of parents.

What do you suppose might happen if a child's "will-to-be-gratified" continued unimpeded into adulthood? That is, if it is human nature to be self-oriented and obsessed with pleasure, what might happen to a child who is not taught self-restraint during the early formative years? What might happen if he is indulged with that for which he cries, pouts, and sulks? How might a child turn out whose parents do not teach him to wait patiently for what he wants, or who is never forced to suffer through the common hardships of childhood, such as picking up his toys or eating whatever food his parents choose for him? Might not such a child grow up with an over-exalted sense of his own importance; and, consequently, a grand sense of entitlement, little gratefulness, and minimal ability to delay gratification? What might happen to a child permitted to escape the consequences of his actions, whose parents clean up his messes and pay for the windows he breaks?

21

And if the same is true for most of his friends and classmates, might they not share a consensus that pursuit of personal pleasure without consequence is their supreme right?

Children start off life with a will-to-be-gratified, and if it is not brought in check when they are young they will arrive at adulthood with the same self-focused, passion-driven worldview they had as toddlers. This outlook on life will affect their relationships with their families, their employers, and their communities. It will also determine their approach to politics and government.

I would like to offer what will be a radical thought for many, but which forms the basis for understanding this book—at the very core of liberalism is *passion*. A liberal perspective, at the deepest level, is rooted in the *heart*—not the *mind*. The liberal mindset stems from *emotions* and *feelings*, which might include compassion for the needy, but more universally expresses itself in the desire for gratification, along with a refusal to suffer the consequences of those desires.

Obviously, some will disagree with my assertion about human nature. They believe that people are born basically good-hearted, and that children grow up to be upstanding citizens if they are permitted independence and reared in love, with minimal restriction or restraint. Yes, this is a common belief in modern America, but it is one that has been proven wrong. The present low moral state of our society reveals that this approach, which has arisen largely since the 1960s, does not work. The proof is all around us.

Pure liberals, of course, will take issue with that. They do not see our society as a place in moral decline—to them America is a place of accelerated human advancement. As a guest on radio talk shows, I have spoken with many who challenge the belief that America is on a downward moral slide. For them a high divorce rate is not a sign of the breakdown of family, but merely liberation from archaic restrictive values. Out-of-wedlock pregnancies and the rampant spread of STDs are not signs of low morals, but are merely unfortunate side effects of healthy sexual liberty (chiefly for those who neglect to practice safe sex). A high rate of abortion is not a sign of disregard for human life, but an indication that women have finally achieved equality with men. To the purest liberals, even the growth of the pornography industry is not a tragedy, but merely proof that we have shaken off our prudish Victorian heritage and are enjoying the freedom of expression provided by the First Amendment. Yes, to the pure liberal, on these counts America is in a good place. Of course, liberals are concerned about our society in areas such as education, substance abuse, health, and care for the needy. My concern, however, lies in the liberal approach to solving those problem areas, which I will address later in the book.

Once again, I know there will be some who call themselves liberals who insist my characterizations don't describe them. They believe that divorce is bad for our culture, and wish there were less fornication, abortion, and pornography. They will accuse me of setting up straw men to topple. I want to suggest to them however, that they are not the *pure* liberals about whom I am writing. Pure liberals and pure conservatives are at polar ends of the spectrum. The majority of America is a blend of both perspectives. My hope is to expose the heart of liberalism to the majority in the middle in order to help them walk away from elements that are harmful to our government and to their children.

Basic Goal of Parenting

If there are so many conservatives and professing liberals who want to raise children with good character, why isn't it happening on a larger scale? One foundational reason is that parents may want to cultivate good character in their children, but most are blind to the ways in which they model the opposite and foster self-absorption in their children. They may sincerely love their children and strive to bring them up with strong character. With the exception of Al and Peg Bundy,[3] few say to themselves, "Let's raise our kid to be a rebel who grows up to look at pornography, lie to his customers, and cheat on his taxes." What is missing for the multitude of so many earnest parents is not love and sacrifice. What is absent is an accurate picture of the good character spoken of by our Founding Fathers and the proper avenue for cultivating it. Until we have a clear destination, we will never arrive.

The virtue and good morality our Founding Fathers emphasized can be wrapped up in one word: MATURITY. Although children grow up, few arrive at adulthood *mature* these days. The passion-to-be-gratified that ruled them as toddlers thrived throughout childhood and exploded in adolescence. They may finally achieve grown-up status, but they lack the character our society so desperately needs from its adult citizens.

"But," some may object, *"how can you say such a thing! Children grow up so fast these days."* Oh, do they? Are teens really grown-up, or are they just independent? The typical modern teen is disrespectful, self-absorbed, and ungrateful—they are preoccupied with entertainment, fun, and pleasure. They manifest the traits of *immaturity*, not maturity. Yes, modern teenagers are more sexually experienced and worldly wise than previous generations, and, yes, they are more sophisticated in their humor than the teens of 1955, but they are far less self-restraining and responsible—key aspects of true maturity. Parents with outspoken, pushy daughters say things like, *"My daughter is thirteen going on twenty,"* but that daughter, based on her insolence, would better be described as *"thirteen going on five."*

America's growing proclivity to produce self-absorbed, irresponsible (immature) adults has concerned social observers for several decades. In an often-quoted speech at Harvard Law School in 1972, Ralph Nader noted:

> We have the most prolonged adolescence in the history of mankind. There is no other society that requires so many years to pass before people are grown up…. Adolescence is nurtured and prolonged by educational processes and by industry that has found a bonanza in embracing the adolescent population and fortifying "adolescent values." This prolongation of adolescence robs the country of the population group having the most risk takers, and the highest ideals.[4]

Similarly, one of my sociology professors in college asserted that our modern culture keeps children young longer than any culture in history. He observed that in almost all world cultures, up until the twentieth century, young people were groomed to mature earlier—in their teens they were in their careers and marrying.[5] It was his contention that the maturity of a typical fifteen-year-old in centuries past was beyond the maturity of an average thirty-year-old *now*.

Needless to say, my professor's words were provocative and stirred me to further study. In subsequent years I did my own research and concluded that what he said was true.

In nineteenth century America and earlier, the average fifteen-year-old was engaged in what we consider adult responsibilities. Take for example John Quincy Adams, who started his political career at age eleven traveling as a diplomatic assistant in Europe; he then served as an ambassadorial assistant in Russia at the age of fourteen. David Farragut, the famed nineteenth century maritime officer, started his naval career at age nine and was given command of a captured British vessel at twelve. Laura Ingalls Wilder was a public school teacher at fifteen. The maturity that earned these three adolescents positions of adult responsibility was not unique among young people, but was typical of most teens throughout world history. Even in our modern era, young people raised in third world cultures demonstrate a similar early maturity.

I have become convinced that there are many contributing factors in the slow maturing of today's young people, including extended education, the commercialization of youth, and low cultural expectations, but the chief cause is inadequate parenting. Most parents do not understand what maturity is or how to develop it in their children.

What Is Maturity?

The foundational goal of parenting is to raise children to be *mature*. The problem in modern America is that most parents assume that maturity is a by-product of getting older. Consequently, few make significant efforts to develop it within their children. In fact, most would have difficulty even defining maturity, and, therefore, are unable to effectively cultivate it. Parents who do want to help their kids become mature often confuse maturity with "independence" and grant their immature children autonomy early in life. They do not realize that an immature person granted independence does not develop the self-restraint of maturity, but regresses deeper into the self-indulgence of *immaturity*. They may develop survival skills and increase in sophistication, but they will not grow in maturity.

Parents must, therefore, understand maturity and make a conscious effort to train their children in its attributes. Maturity, broken down to its most basic elements, can be characterized by three primary character traits: *self-control, wisdom,* and *responsibility*.[6]

A *self-controlled* person has all normal human passions, but is not ruled by them. A self-controlled child is one who is able to obey Mommy the first time when called. It is a self-controlled child who is able to not touch something that belongs to others or not sneak candy when Daddy's back is turned. Such a child may be angered when teased, but will have the self-restraint to not respond with violence. The bottom line is that a child with self-control has the ability to say "no" to himself and "yes" to what is right. The child who is allowed to grow up without self-restraint may reach adulthood, but will remain a big "kid"—absorbed with himself, pleasure, fun, and entertainment, sometimes at the expense of those around him. Whatever he thinks or feels is of supreme importance, and he, therefore, will be prone to saying whatever is on his mind, whether respectful or not, and will pursue whatever appeals to his passions. His self-centeredness will make him arrogant, impatient, demanding, and ungrateful. He will be unable to easily delay gratification. One without self-restraint will lack a mature, selfless concern for others, which is critical for a healthy society.

A *wise* person is not the same as a *smart* person whose intelligence is innate. Many highly educated, brilliant people make foolish choices every day—their rational thinking skills are impaired by their passions and drives. A person who is truly wise is one who learns from mistakes, makes sound decisions, and handles stressful problems with a level head. More importantly, people with wisdom are *rational*, because passions are not clouding their thinking. For example, when our craving for illicit sexual experiences causes us to pursue gratification without regard to the consequences, we have not acted in wisdom, but in fact, have become quite the fool. When our craving for alcohol is so great that we sneak to hide our booze and lie to cover our actions, even when sober we make foolish choices that affect everyone around us.

When our compulsion to play the lottery or to buy that new dress causes us to spend money that should have been spent on rent, we and others suffer from our unwise choices. Unless a child is raised to say "no" to his passions or whims, he will never walk in the wisdom necessary for maturity. In fact, because that which rules us colors our outlook on life, the child and others raised like him will see life through the cloudy eyes of passion. He will view himself as insightful and wise, when in actuality, he is the opposite, because his perspective is skewed by his passions.

A *responsible* person is one who accepts personal accountability for his own actions. He does not make excuses or blame others for his failures, and does not expect others to pay the consequences for his mistakes. He takes responsibility for himself and pays his own bills in life. A responsible person is faithful and conscientious in work habits. Such integrity and reliability, however, are only possible when passions are not in charge. When a child's desire for fun is greater than his sense of duty, he will compulsively play when it is time to work, and when he grows up he will produce poorly for his employer. When a child is not held responsible to fulfill his personal duties, but is given "another chance" time and again, he grows up thinking that everyone else is responsible to bail him out. He thinks he should not have to live with the consequences of his actions, and comes to develop a "victim" mentality—nothing is ever his fault—someone else is always to blame for his misery. He sees himself as not responsible for the results of his choices or of his reactions to life. In fact, he insists he has a right to that which he has not earned and is entitled to be given that for which others have worked.

So the primary goal of parenting is to raise children to be *mature*, having the traits of *self-control*, *wisdom*, and *responsibility*. The young person whose life reflects these traits will be ready for adulthood, and the society whose citizens reflect such character will be benefited as well. Many parents of the last fifty years have not made instilling these traits their primary goal, so their children have grown up and become politicians, judges, and civil servants who lead us just as their parents led them. Today our nation reaps the bad fruit of that leadership.

CHAPTER FOUR

RAISING GOOD CITIZENS

"The emotional indulgence of parents today is depriving children the opportunity to learn through adversity. Most adolescents from affluent families have all the useful accessories—cell phones, credit cards, computers, and cars—but they have few of the responsibilities that build character.... Indulged children become susceptible to self-absorption, depression, anxiety, and lack of self control."

—Ed Shipman[1]

ONE DAY AT A PARENTING SEMINAR, a single mother ran up to me and excitedly explained she had attended a seminar I had conducted a year earlier. She had two preadolescent sons and had come to the event weary from competing with them for control of her home. Beaming, she told me that she left the seminar with permission to be a parent. Within one day, she watched her home transform. Her sons stopped sassing her and began obeying the first time she spoke. She was happier and so were the boys. She was more at peace because she no longer had to repeat herself and her sons no longer competed with her for control—they accepted that she was the leader and they were the followers. Until then, she had always just tried to *survive* her sons—now she saw her job was to develop their character and prepare them for their adult lives. She was delighted when she discovered that she had power to influence who they were becoming.

So how do parents shape their children's character and groom them with self-control, wisdom, and responsibility? I have written an entire book on that subject, so I will not take space here to duplicate that work.[2] However, to lay a foundation for evaluating politics and culture, I will summarize ten basic principles for raising children to maturity and good citizenship.

Let me say, before I continue, that I am speaking about proper ways to *train* our children, with emphasis on the word *train*. Some people are offended by the concept of *training* children. *"Training,"* they insist, *"is what you do with dogs. Children are not dogs!"* Children are definitely not animals, and should not be treated like them. *Training*, however, is something we all need as people, especially when simple *instruction* is inadequate. *Instruction* involves dispensing of information—*training* is more intensive and secures a better outcome. That is why employers sponsor *on-the-job training* for their employees, coaches prescribe *fitness training* for their athletes, and the military requires *basic training* for our soldiers. Instruction of children is critical for their development, but instruction must be reinforced by practice, role-playing, and discipline—all aspects of training. Without proper training a child may age, but will not reach maturity.

1. Children must be helped to bring their passions in check.

Children start off life with a will-to-be-gratified. If that will is allowed to continue unchecked, a child will grow up ruled by his passions. A person ruled by his passions will make decisions based not on wisdom or responsibility, but on what gratifies. Such a person will not be governed by objective logic or a commitment to personal integrity, but by what is expedient. He will fight to ensure he and others like him have continued access to that which gratifies, and will try to obligate others to rescue him from the consequences of his choices. To prevent such an outcome, the primary goal of parental training must be to help children learn self-control.

A few years ago, I flew to a conference on Southwest Airlines, which has no assigned seats. I happened to have boarded first and took a seat a few rows from the front. As I sat waiting for the rest of the passengers to board, I observed a tired mom get on with two sons about ten and eleven years old. As she headed down the aisle, the two boys stopped at the two front seats that happened to face each other, and called out to their mother that they wanted to sit there. Apparently having no interest in playing footsie with the passengers she would have to face, Mom told the boys "no" and instructed them to follow her towards the back. The boys obviously knew how to work their mother, so they stood their ground, begging and pointing to the front-row seats. I watched, curious to see if she would obey them. Sure enough, they had trained her well; after a little verbal tit-for-tat she finally gave in and trudged back up to the row in which she did not want to sit.

This mother was representative of so many families in America run not by the parents, but by those least qualified to take charge—the children. It is no surprise that the Duke of Windsor once famously remarked that what impressed him most in America was the way parents obey their children.[3]

Families are organizations with two basic roles for the members—parent/leaders and child/followers. It is the job of the older, wiser leaders to direct and equip the youthful, inexperienced followers. It is the responsibility of the followers not to help lead, but to receive the leadership provided by their parents. As the followers learn to say, "Yes, Mom and Dad," and do exactly what they are told, they are being equipped to be leaders themselves some day. The military learned long ago that the best followers make the best leaders—*group consensus* destroys effectiveness.

Children, because of their innate desire for gratification, do not need to *exercise* leadership, but to *follow* strong leadership. Parents are there to give them mastery over their passions. Such training is really not too complicated—small children learn self-control by having to say "no" to themselves and "yes" to their parents. *Inner* controls are developed by submitting to *outer* controls.[4] We, therefore, must offer our children strong leadership for the first few years of their life, giving them little say in the decisions we make for them. They must *not* be included as a part of the husband-wife parental leadership team, not only because they need to learn the self-denial which comes from doing what they are told, but because psychologically, their small shoulders cannot handle the stress of helping to run the home. Young children permitted a constant voice in parental decisions are typically not happy. But once relieved of such duties, they generally become secure and at peace. The weight is lifted from them when it is obvious someone else is in charge.

Children raised to think they should have a say in all decisions that affect them grow up self-centered, demanding, impatient, and ungrateful. They are so absorbed with what they think is best for *them*, at the exclusion of *others*, that they are often discontent, critical, and prone to complaining. Parents who encourage their child to always speak his mind may never have to second-guess his opinions, but they inadvertently feed his contempt for authority.

Parents who allow children to jump into parental leadership discussions will discover that the children develop the mindset that they are their parents' peers, and it is their right to help direct the home. Such familiarity inevitably breeds contempt, thereby causing a parent to lose the respect of their children. Sadly, the children grow up despising the ones in the best position to train and instruct them.

Parents are certainly wise to solicit the thoughts and opinions of their children, especially as they head into adolescence. After all, we love our children—they are our flesh and blood. They are *people* and deserve the respect of having their thoughts and feelings heard. However, the family is not a democracy—parents are the leaders, and children are the followers. Our country may have democratic elections, but few employers offer employees a vote. So we must teach our children to submit to authority while they are young. Childhood is a season of learning to accept leadership with grace and humility. During this season not only do our children learn self-discipline from submitting to leadership, but that self-discipline equips them to become capable leaders themselves someday. Strong parental leadership, of course, necessitates that parents themselves have a strong moral base.

2. Children's happiness must not be the driving force of the home.

Yes, we love our children and want them to be happy, but preoccupation with "happy" children is helping to bring down our culture. Our homes, our schools, and our communities have become *child-centered*—we pander to their desire for fun and gratification, wanting them kept happy at any cost. This has resulted in our children's will-to-be-gratified thriving into adulthood, and has created a culture of teens and adults with an exalted sense of their own importance. With the priority everyone has given their gratification, they have come to believe the world revolves around them.

Do not misconstrue what I am saying—I want children to be happy. Nothing uplifts me more than seeing a joyful child laugh and smile, particularly my own. What I am saying is that we must not *live* to gratify our children's desires and make our leadership decisions based on their responses. In my years of traveling the country presenting parenting seminars, the happiest children I've seen are always those who are secure under their parents' loving authority. They obey the first time they are spoken to, and know they will be rewarded with the trust of their parents when they obey or reap a disciplinary consequence if they disobey. They are happy, because they find safety within the boundaries established and enforced by their parents. They are at peace because they do not have to carry the load of helping their parents run the home. Needless to say, homes with secure and peaceful children have far less strife and sibling rivalry—they are happier places to be. None of this should be a surprise—our children are just like us—stress is minimized when we believe someone else is shouldering responsibility.

3. Children must not be indulged.

As parents we want to give our children control over their will-to-be-gratified, but indulging them with everything for which they beg, cry, or pout does the opposite. Indulging them may include keeping their closet full of the latest fashions, buying them the newest video games, or getting them a cell phone with unlimited minutes. We indulge them when we offer freedom to do whatever they want, whenever they want, with minimal accountability. We indulge them when we permit them to talk back and voice their opinions about every instruction they receive. And we inflate their sense of self-importance when we make all family decisions based *not* on what we think is wisest or best, but on their moods and reactions. An indulged child effectively runs his home.

One of the side effects of habitually gratifying our children's desires for pleasure is that it creates in them a sense of entitlement, which will be accompanied by a general lack of appreciation. Indulged children are difficult to please—their moments of happiness are often fleeting. And when they are not pleased they can make everyone around them miserable, too. Many parents think that such attitudes are simply unavoidable aspects of growing up. They have no idea that these attitudes are fostered by lax or indulgent parenting.

An attitude of appreciativeness is found in children who are humble, who understand the cost of what they have been given, and who realize they have done nothing to earn it. Children who have been given control over their self-centered nature grow up with a great sense of personal responsibility and no sense of entitlement.

The truth is that life does not give us everything we want. It is unfair, then, to buy for our children everything we can afford, and then send them into life ill-equipped for its realities. They will either go deep into debt trying to maintain the lifestyle they learned at home, or they will live in a state of discontent and depend on others to make life better for them. Ultimately, many children today in affluent America are what used to be called "spoiled" children. They grow up thinking that their parents and the world owe them what they crave. If you think about it, *spoiled* means *ruined*.

4. Children must not be rescued from every hardship.

When our children are infants we listen to their cries to know when they are suffering some discomfort and need our attention. As I stated in Chapter Three, their will-to-survive manifests as a will-to-be-gratified the older they get. The problem is that many parents never distinguish the difference, and although their children grow older, they continue to rescue them every time they cry, pout, or grumble.

Such "rescuing" might mean they permit the children to complain ungratefully about what they have been served for dinner, or worse, Mom goes back to the stove and cooks them something else. "Rescuing" may mean parents jump to provide entertainment in response to every complaint of boredom. Perhaps they never require the kids to wait patiently for attention, but instead reward their whining and complaining by stopping immediately to give them what they want—and they even apologize when they force them to wait. It even may mean they cut the bread crusts from their children's sandwiches. To be sure, the children will have to face the bread crusts of life eventually.

Overprotection of our children can mean we run to defend them from anything that might leave them feeling badly about themselves. This might be a sports league that emphasizes winning, a school grading system that might allow them to feel they've failed, or words such as "wrong" or "bad." Whenever their feelings are hurt by a playmate we do our children no favor when we rush to their defense and attack the offender. Parents must protect children from harm. However, we harm them ourselves if we do not teach them how to endure offenses and handle the inevitable "difficult people" in life. We must model for them that other people's words or opinions of us need not determine how we react.

The old adage *"sticks and stones may break my bones, but words will never hurt me"* seems to have been forgotten. By their defensiveness many modern parents reinforce to their children that words are devastating. Let us raise our children to use kind words themselves, but let us also teach them pity for those who do not speak kindly. If we are not careful we will raise our children to be thin-skinned social wimps who blame others for their own inability to handle offenses.

Another way parents overprotect their children is to exempt them from work around the house. Some parents rationalize that childhood is a time of leisure and fun, kind of "one big recess" before children grow up and have to face the challenges of life.

These parents figure that schoolwork provides enough work for kids, and so they minimize or eliminate chores, or any other responsibilities their children might face.

Such parents are deeply confused about parental love. They instinctively feel compelled to nurture and protect, yet their "protection" indulges and effectively harms their children. Learning to face and overcome life's hardships is a key part of developing maturity. Any experienced athlete will confirm that principle—growth comes through facing challenges, not avoiding them. Parents who rescue their children from the trials of life foster laziness and self-absorption. But even worse, they miss the key season for grooming children for adulthood. Childhood is not to be one big recess before adulthood—it is to be the season for preparation for adulthood and all its responsibilities. We must not rescue our children every time they complain, and we must raise them to understand that all who live in a home are responsible to maintain it—at the least, they need daily chores.[5] These things are imperative for the development of maturity.

5. Children must be allowed to suffer the consequences of their actions.

Parental love compels us to nurture and care for our children. We want to protect them from all suffering. The problem is that misapplied love can be harmful to our children's development. When we continually rescue them from having to suffer the consequences of their actions, we keep them from developing a proper sense of personal responsibility. We accidentally foster immaturity by doing for our children that which they are able and *need* to do for themselves.

Responsible people are not only reliable to do their duties, but do not depend upon others to clean up their messes or pay for their obligations. When our children make a mess, they must be required to clean it up. When they break something, they need to repair or replace it. Restoration and restitution are key expressions of personal responsibility.

If our child leaves his bike out in the front yard, despite our warnings, and it is stolen, we must not run off and buy him another one. Children will learn responsibility by having to save their money to buy another one themselves. If they damage a toy belonging to a friend, they must buy a new one whether asked to or not. Parental defensiveness at these times feels so right, but is damaging to our children. From the time they are young we must reinforce to them that it is their duty to clean up their own messes, repair what they damage, and pay their own bills in life, including their own parking tickets and traffic fines.

If we do not hold our children accountable for themselves, but rescue them from the consequences of their actions, they grow up to believe that pursuit of personal pleasure without consequence is their supreme right. They develop a "victim" mentality, thinking that they are not responsible for the circumstances that they have brought upon themselves. In fact, they become convinced that someone else is to blame for their distress, and thus it becomes someone else's duty to take care of their problems.

In addition, parents accidentally teach children irresponsibility by issuing too many warnings or by reinforcing bad behavior. When a child is caught sneaking dessert before dinner, parents encourage bad behavior by merely admonishing him not to do it again, and allowing him to finish eating what he took. That is no different than teachers who consistently permit students to turn in assignments past the due date, without penalty. Consistently allowing children to behave irresponsibly without consequence encourages future misconduct. In fact, such leniency cultivates the perspective that mercy is *owed* them.

A victim mentality is also cultivated by excusing children for wrong reactions to others. If Mark punches his brother Billy because Billy called him a bad name, we must not excuse Mark's violent reaction and accuse Billy of provoking his brother. Billy must be held accountable for his words and Mark must be held accountable for his reactions. Both are 100 percent responsible for their own behavior. If we get in the habit of excusing our children's reaction to others' words, they will grow up without emotional resilience, and easily take offense at mere words. Our children must learn from our instruction and our example that our reaction is our responsibility, and that it is a demonstration of maturity to overlook an offense. If we do not, they will grow up as "victims" or follow our example as "enablers."

6. Children must be required to obey the first time they are spoken to.

In order for children to gain mastery over their will-to-be-gratified they must be trained to do exactly what their parents tell them. This means that parental directives must be spoken calmly and only one time, with an appropriate disciplinary consequence for disobedience.[6] Children trained this way from the time they are toddlers typically gain the ability to control themselves fairly quickly, and need comparatively little disciplinary consequences from the time they are five years old. Based on our knowledge of parenting customs from earlier centuries, this is the manner in which most of our Founding Fathers were raised, and formed the basis for their own development of character.

An important key to remember is that parents must give directives just once. If they hear themselves saying things such as, *"I've told you a hundred times..."* or *"How many times must I tell you...?"* they should not be surprised that their children disregard them. From the perspective of the children, all the repeated directives are just warnings, and they are postponing obedience until Mom or Dad "really means business." The profound truth is that if children can obey after the fifth time—they demonstrate that they do have the capacity to obey. Parents must recognize this and stop the repetition with all its negative fallout.

When an authority figure habitually repeats directives or gives multiple warnings, it produces several negative side effects:

> 1. Children permitted to continually disregard instructions grow up with their will-to-be-gratified alive and well.
>
> 2. Children consistently permitted to disregard their parents' voices will lack the capacity to obey quickly at the threat of danger, such as scenarios involving hot pans, vicious dogs, or traffic.

3. Those that have authority, but are reluctant to exercise it, foster disrespect in those they lead. Their authority, in fact, becomes a joke. Parents who lose their children's respect can often trace it back to this.

4. Children learn to disregard instructions, effectively training them to disobey. Parents should not get angry with their child for not obeying the first time, when they, by their constant repetition, taught him they could be disregarded until they showed they "meant business."

5. When parents repeat themselves, their anger may build until they are driven by rage to bring punishment. Raging parents can be tempted toward abusive parenting.

7. Children must be taught to obey without always knowing the reason why.

If parents establish firm behavioral boundaries for their toddlers, not offering a reason why they should obey, and limiting their personal choices, these children, by the time they are four years old, will have learned self-denial and be well on the path to self-control. A self-governed four-year-old has accepted his parents' authority and is prepared to *begin* hearing the wise reasons behind Mommy and Daddy's directives. If children are offered reasons to obey before they have learned to obey without them, they will not learn the self-denial that is the foundation for self-control.

Do not misunderstand me; to grow in wisdom, children must be taught the reasoning behind parental commands. The time in childhood to begin making them wise, however, is only after they have demonstrated they can consistently obey without needing to know why. When that time comes, parents must not give lengthy explanations to *convince* a child that he needs to obey. The plan is to state a simple nugget of wisdom along with the parental directive. A full explanation is not to be given at the moment a child is expected to obey. Children must learn that they are to obey first, and then return for the full reason. Parents who think they will gain better cooperation if they provide reasons along with their commands discover such discussion is perceived as an invitation to debate.

Sassy and argumentative children who think that parents owe them convincing explanations usually get that way because parents justify all their instructions. Children raised in such homes tend to grow up insubordinate toward teachers, law enforcement officers, employers, and others in positions of authority.

8. Children must be required to treat parents and other adults with respect.

We live in an age when respect for authority has all but disappeared. When I was young, my friends and I had been taught by our parents that we were to respect our elders. We did not see ourselves as the social equals of adults, so we never dreamed of calling them by their first names. When anyone in authority spoke, we listened and responded in a way that showed no contempt for their position. I recall only once or twice seeing a student "talk back" to a teacher in my K-12 school years. During the student protests in the late 1960s I was stunned by the insubordination toward authority shown by university students on the evening news—I could not relate. As I look back I realize that America was beginning to reap the fruit of indulgent parenting. It is no surprise that just as young people were starting to show disrespect for authority, the crime rate was crawling up as well.

Respect for all authority, whether it is for people or rules, is learned at home. Being required to obey parents and communicate respectfully teaches self-restraint and emphasizes that not everything one feels or thinks need be expressed. It reinforces the self-control inherent to maturity, and helps children grow up to be good citizens.[7]

9. Children need parental oversight of their moral diet.

As parents we instinctively protect our young. When they are infants we feed them nutritious foods and rescue them from diaper rash; we sterilize their bottles and guard their need for sleep. We teach them to walk, and then keep them away from sharp objects, the fireplace, and dogs that bite. But as they grow older, their desire for gratification increases, and they begin to resist our efforts to shelter them. Many parents are insecure in their authority, so they become intimidated and afraid to stay firm when their children fight them. Against their better judgment, these parents permit their children involvement with questionable entertainment and activities.

By virtue of their years and life experience, parents have a greater understanding of cause and effect than their children. They know the wisdom behind statements such as, *"Eat your spinach," "You need your sleep,"* and *"Stay out of the street."* All a child knows is that he craves junk food, likes to stay up late, and the street seems a fun place to play. Because the average child has little life experience and his thinking is clouded by his "will-to-be-gratified," he is the last person to know what is good for him. Parents must realize that they do not need their children's permission to be "parents" — they already have that role. They must simply act on their authority, without apology. Children will not protect themselves from their appetites, so parents must take charge and protect them physically, mentally, and morally.

For anyone uncertain of children's need for moral protection, I want to remind them that our values are greatly influenced by what we see and hear. Madison Avenue figured this out a long time ago, and annually profits billions of dollars manipulating people's values. The government and people in the entertainment industry understand it, too. That's why music, video games, and movies are regulated with age-appropriate ratings. Children are judged to have a measure of innocence that would be lost if they were exposed to immoral stimulation. Not only does sensuality, vulgarity, or graphic violence rob children of innocence, but excessive exposure desensitizes them and cultivates unhealthy appetites.

I have been collecting studies on the impact of the entertainment media for more than thirty years. The studies overwhelmingly show that what we read, watch, and listen to impacts what we value and how we live. It might be said that our lives bear the fruit of the seeds we plant. Children who saturate themselves with entertainment marked by senseless violence will be more tolerant or prone to violence; those who watch movies or music videos containing sensuality will increasingly express themselves sexually; children or adults with a diet of entertainment involving illicit relationships will treat marriage and wedding vows with less honor. We should not be surprised that as America's children have developed an appetite for questionable entertainment, the country has sunk to moral lows. The bottom line is that parents must decide who they will permit to plant seeds in their children's lives.

It is important to note that by itself, sheltering does not create character. It merely protects a child from negative influences during his most formative years—the years his parents are supposed to be actively shaping his character. A child's character is formed primarily by what *good* goes into him, and not only by what is kept from him. And no one is in a position to sow into his life like Mom and Dad. Unlimited use of computers, video games, television, and MP3 players is standard diversion for kids these days. But these electronic babysitters are cheap, sometimes harmful, substitutes for time with Mom and Dad. Therefore, parents must decide that their children are worth a daily investment of time and should use that time for building character.

10. Children must be loved.

Most parents instinctively love their children. However, not all express their love in constructive ways. As I have sought to point out, some inadvertently harm their children by equating love with indulgence. Others erroneously think it is love to remove all pain and hardships and rescue children from the consequences of their choices. Still others think they love their children when they habitually withhold or soften discipline. And even more subtly, some think love is *giving* in order to receive affection and loyalty in return. Just because parents have warm feelings of affection for their child does not mean that the child grows up benefiting from that affection.

Parental love means doing what is best for children no matter how they might respond. One of the reasons modern parents are so soft on their children is that they crave their acceptance. They are unlike parents in past generations who did not need their kids to like them. Parents more than fifty years ago knew that life was hard, and in an effort to prepare their children for life, they did not tolerate whining or complaining. Somehow, America has raised a crop of insecure parents who fear their children's rejection. These parents are afraid to let their children cry. They are scared to make them mad. And they dread the thought that their kids will hate them. These parents, therefore, do all they can to make them happy, and try to win their affection. Such parental love is not love at all. When we give to our children to get affection back, we are not *loving* them—we are *using* them to elicit good feelings about ourselves.

The bottom line is that when our children are young and vulnerable, they absolutely need our leadership if they are to grow up to maturity. If we look to them for value and significance, we are not truly leading them—we are *following* them—much like politicians pandering to voters, hoping to be reelected. True parental love requires self-sacrifice. I do not just mean the sacrifice we manifest as we nurse them through the night when they are sick, or when we give up our Saturdays to take them to soccer. I speak of the sacrifice required to risk loss of popularity. To selflessly love our children means being willing to make decisions or administer discipline no matter what their reaction.

Some parents cannot relate to those who strive for their children's acceptance. They have read this chapter and feel really good about themselves and their parenting. So for those self-assured, firm parents I have one more admonition about loving children. I want to caution you. I have found that it is possible to intimidate children into subjection, but fail to win their hearts into submission. This means that children may submit to discipline and controls, and listen respectfully when parents speak, but their hearts will be far away. A parent who does not have their child's heart will eventually discover that all the compliance and respect is simply an expression of *self-preservation*. Such a child may patronize his parents and outwardly honor them during his early teen years, but flee their authoritarian rule the first chance he gets. The self-discipline and virtue he appeared to have may not go as deeply into his character as his parents had hoped. I've heard from hundreds of parents whose seemingly model children grew up and went astray.

Intense, consistent parents, who implement the first nine principles I have outlined, will see children develop self-control and respect for authority. However influencing *behavior* is not the same as influencing *hearts*. Parents who are able to maintain influence over their children's hearts, which is critical in the teen years, are those who have cultivated rich, loving relationships with their children. In the military, establishment of rules without love is effective, but in a *family*, rules-without-relationship is a recipe for disaster. Intense parents who hold high standards for their homes must be especially careful to not make good behavior their only goal. Parents who want to influence *who their teenage children are* and not just *what they do* must love and accept them for who they are, whether they live up to standards or not. After all, our children are just like us—they are drawn to those who accept them. When they look into our eyes, they must see that we value them. And if they fail, they must see that our love and acceptance have not changed.[8]

I want to emphasize that this summary of basic parenting principles is by no means exhaustive and should not be relied upon as a complete guideline. Anyone who desires help with rearing children should listen to my parenting seminar "Biblical Insights into Child Training" and read my book *Child Training Tips: What I wish I knew when my children were young*.[9] In this chapter I have covered these foundational principles strictly to demonstrate how political philosophies are rooted in the way in which people are parented. Those who would like to stop and test their ability to identify parenting that produces liberalism can turn to Appendix A and read the scenario "The Story of Junior."

To summarize, character, formed in childhood, is a key element of true maturity. If we want our children to flourish in the academic disciplines of school, we need to send them there with self-discipline. If we want to reduce crime and get our people to stop stealing, they must be trained as children to respect others' personal property. If we want to eliminate violence in our homes, schools, and communities, we must give our children self-control and rear them to love their families, friends, and enemies. If we want to diminish the number of broken homes, we must model the sanctity of marriage for our own children. If we want to reduce out-of-wedlock pregnancies and STDs, our children must learn from us to be self-restrained and to value purity. For children to grow up to be good citizens who take responsibility for themselves, parents must assume their position as parents and give their children the leadership they so desperately need.

CHAPTER FIVE

GOVERNING WITH THE *HEART*, NOT THE *HEAD*

"Any man who is under thirty and is not a Liberal has no heart; and any man who is over thirty and not a Conservative has no brains."

—Winston Churchill[1]

IT HAS BEEN MY GOAL TO DEMONSTRATE that by nature we are all born self-oriented and obsessed with pleasure. If left to our natural tendencies, we grow up with an exalted sense of our own importance, a grand sense of entitlement, little gratefulness, and minimal ability to delay gratification. Subsequently, our view of life will be filtered chiefly through our emotions and feelings— ultimately through our passions. Thoughts filtered through passion are not consistently logical.

I can recall admiring my buddies' new squirt guns one day when I was about ten years old. I had no squirt gun, but I saw the amazing power they could give a guy. I wanted one badly—so badly that I was willing to violate my conscience to get one. First, I stole my father's loose change from the top of his dresser. Then, I rode my bike to the drug store to see which model I could afford. The one I set my heart on was a huge revolver. It must have held three times as much water as any I had seen in the hands of my friends. I knew the threat I would pose and the envy I would earn with that gun, but it cost more money than I had. I was so obsessed with that weapon, I decided to switch its price tag with the less expensive model. I had never done anything like this before, so in trepidation I walked to the counter, paid seventy-nine cents for the gun, rode home, but was never caught. I had stolen from my own father, shoplifted, and risked arrest, all because I thought I had to have the object of my desire. Passion can make us do things we think morally impossible for us, as a child or as an adult.

Most of us are aware of the power of passion to cloud our thinking. A few minutes of sexual passion and we end up with an unplanned pregnancy or infected with an STD. A moment of rage and we commit violence or speak words we later regret. An obsession with getting what we want and we make rash or foolish choices to obtain it. Lust, rage, anger, jealousy, covetousness, greed, pride, and fear are powerful influences over the human mind. When such passions are allowed free expression from childhood we grow up not the master of our passions, but their servant. In other words, our worldview and thinking processes are not clear and logical, but are filtered through the cloudy thoughts of passion and feelings. This in turn shapes our view of government and determines our political associations as well.

As I have contended, this passion-orientation is a key element of liberalism. Those with a liberal worldview are children who have grown up without seeing the harm of feeding one's passions. Don't get me wrong—I am not suggesting that all liberals are completely undisciplined in their habits, or that every professing liberal is a total hedonist. Not at all—few people are *purely* anything. What I am saying is that liberal *thought* is passion-based, as a result of childhood influences. Those with a liberal worldview therefore, tend to develop hedonistic political philosophies and an approach to government that will ensure that they can secure the rights to pursue pleasure and gratification for themselves and others like them. This is why liberals are preoccupied with the right to unrestricted free expression. It is their means of protecting their freedom to do what they want—no matter how trivial, how base, or how immoral. It is no surprise therefore, that overtly passion-driven people are drawn to liberal political parties, including the sexually promiscuous, criminals, pornographers, and drug users.

Philosophy and Passion Trump Reason

Because a liberal's thinking tends to be clouded by his passions, everything is processed from the feelings more than the mind. That is why it is difficult to engage most liberals in a logical debate of facts. They arm themselves with statistics or facts in an effort to bolster their arguments, but their positions often are not actually based on those facts. They are rooted in a pre-established philosophical absolute and a passion-based view of life. As an example, take the issue of abortion.

Liberal feminists state that they must have the right to abortion so that they can maintain equality with men. They contend that if a man does not have to be pregnant, then neither should a woman. This established absolute makes any logical discussion of abortion impossible. No matter what biological facts about the humanity of a pre-born child are presented, or how circumspectly Socratic reasoning is employed, abortion advocates are so committed to their philosophical position that they cannot begin to be open to scientific or rational realities. Although a popular liberal axiom is, *"The mind is like a parachute. It only functions when open,"* their established absolutes keep their minds closed. Liberals don't *want* to know the truth—they can't afford to—there is too much at stake.

The average person who argues for abortion rights does not actually come from the feminist position. People are committed to abortion mostly because it is good for their lifestyle—they do not want to live with the consequences of their sexual actions, and want the same for others. Either that or they have to justify their own past abortion or one they supported. That's why when discussing the subject of abortion, reasonable people suddenly lose their rationality and start spouting emotionally charged platitudes and mottos. Passion craves "freedom" and hates guilt.

In the middle of discussing the facts related to the abortion procedure, I have seen highly intelligent people clap their hands over their ears and start shouting so they did not have to hear what was being said about the abortion procedure. I have attended pro-life rallies and seen abortion advocates stand at their seats to disrupt the event by shouting nonsensical slogans while a speaker testified of the pain and regret from her own abortion. Once, when I was in the middle of an interview with a major TV news station, the reporter became visibly upset. While I was explaining the process of mid- and late-term abortions he blurted out, "I refuse to believe that," and then just turned around while I was mid-sentence and walked away. Most reporters would simply edit out the parts of an interview they did not want—this fellow could not bear even to hear scientific facts he did not like. Reason, logic, and facts are insignificant when passion, gratification, and freedom from responsibility are at stake.

Willful Blindness

Anyone who listens to talk radio is probably aware of the difference between liberal and conservative talk show hosts, not to mention liberal and conservative callers. I was a talk show host in the late 1980s, and I still hear several hours of talk radio each week. There is a distinct difference between liberal and conservative talk shows. If you want to hear passion, intensity, and low blows, listen to liberals. If you want to hear logic and well-thought-out arguments, listen to conservatives. Liberals are as intelligent as conservatives, so they can make reasonable-sounding cases for their positions, but typically their arguments are based not on facts, but on *feelings*. When challenged, passion-driven people are blind to simple logic or facts. Their blindness is not a matter of intellect, but of *will*. They *will* not see, because they have too much to lose, personally. To consider they might be wrong would require that they give up something they depend upon for security. Or it may put them at odds with the liberal leaders they admire and parrot—the ones who fight for their right to pursue their passions.

Liberals are like teenagers whose will-to-be-gratified was never subdued, and now cannot grasp the simple logic of what is being said to them. They are so emotionally obsessed with getting what their hearts want that they are unwilling to listen to reason. That is why liberals resort to personal attacks, name-calling, accusing, yelling, discrediting, or changing the subject. And that is why they use inflammatory and emotionally charged words like "intolerant," "hateful," and "racist." Desperation ensues when passion rules. When passion rules, blindness sets in.

All of us have the potential to be blind at times. That's why we do or say rash things when we are smitten with someone. Later we ask ourselves, *"What was I thinking! Why didn't I listen to friends and family who tried to warn me about this relationship?"* We did not listen because we were temporarily ruled by our hormones and blinded by our emotions. The problem with liberals is that they never got control of their will-to-be-gratified, and live in a state of emotional blindness.

That is why education is not the answer for the promiscuous or for intravenous drug users. Our nation has been saturated with education regarding "safe sex" and clean needles. Yet, it seems to fall on deaf ears—STD and AIDS infection rates continue to climb as multitudes use dirty needles and have "unprotected sex." Passions make you blind and dumb. The problem is in the *heart* not the *head*.

Ronald Reagan, when running for governor of California, described such delusional thinking this way, "The trouble with our liberal friends is not that they're ignorant; it's just that they know so much that isn't so."[2]

Following the Blind over the Cliff

The most frightening aspect of liberal blindness is that through the courts and legislatures they have the power to lead our country farther down the path of moral decline. The thought that people making decisions for our nation are ruled by their passions is unnerving. It has been my observation that one who is a slave to his passions cannot rule his home, for that which rules him, rules his home. When people entrusted with the responsibility to lead are under the influence of someone or something else, their leadership is frightening. They are like a bus driver impaired by alcohol who is bound to crash the bus. Frankly, when liberals are behind the wheel, it is terrifying to be a passenger.

CHAPTER SIX

FREEDOM TO BE ENSLAVED

*"Only a virtuous people are capable of freedom.
As nations become corrupt and vicious, they have more need of masters."*

—Benjamin Franklin[1]

IT WAS 1989 and I was preparing a sermon on the sanctity of human life, so I went to the local copy shop to have some color transparencies made from photos of aborted children. When I laid out the photos on the counter, the young man preparing to take my order stared in shock at the sight of the mangled bodies. When I explained that he was looking at the remains of children killed by abortion, he was overwhelmed. He said he had no idea that children in the womb were fully formed, or that abortion was such a gruesome act. In just a moment he had gone from "pro-choice" to "pro-life." He even called the three young men working with him to come over to take a look, so they could be convinced as well. He was not only suddenly pro-life, but had become an advocate for the unborn.

When I left the copy shop with my transparencies that day I had a new friend. We always chatted when I came in for my photocopy needs, although we never again spoke of abortion. Eventually, he took a job at another shop, and I lost track of him. A few years later, I ran into him at his new job and he took a few minutes to catch me up on his life. He even shared with me how he had almost become a daddy, but had solved that "problem" by talking his girlfriend into getting an abortion. Seeing the shocked look on my face, he realized what he had said, so mumbled some kind of excuse and changed the subject.

Although he believed in his mind that an abortion took the life of a helpless child and was morally wrong, when faced with the challenge of a "problem pregnancy," the child became just a "problem" to be overcome. My friend was ruled not by what he knew to be moral, but by his determination to have a carefree life. The bottom line was that he loved his own life more than the life of his child. Expedience trumped morals.

Freedom or Enslavement?

We are all born into this world with a hedonistic bent in our nature, and it is critical our parents teach us that we need not be ruled by our every whim. If they inadvertently indulge us, and we are allowed to grow up thinking that our own gratification is preeminent, we will reach adulthood with a passion-oriented perspective on life. Our thoughts will not be clear or logical, but filtered through our passions. Consequently, we will hold in the highest regard the freedom to do as we wish.

Liberals hold *individual liberty* as their primary political value. Our nation, of course, was founded to secure individual liberty. Both liberal and conservative Americans cherish that beautiful right. To a liberal, however, individual liberty does not mean the same as to a conservative. For those who have grown up under the influence of their will-to-be-gratified, liberty means to be free to do whatever they want, under the law. They view such liberty as the right to free expression protected by the First Amendment. The Constitution's Framers, however, never envisioned unbridled passion as a liberty or a right to be protected. On the contrary, they believed that our free society could only remain free if the individuals in it were self-governing, with passions in check. What liberals fail to understand is that their view of freedom is actually *enslavement*, for when passions rule us, we are not free at all.

The "freedoms" that liberals fight so hard to maintain are harmful to individuals and to society at large. Since *they* typically do not like to say "no" to themselves, and neither do most of their constituents, they assume that everyone is just like them. They remember as teens not having the power of self-restraint, so they resist efforts to teach teenagers abstinence in schools. They argue that that is expecting too much. Liberals would much rather encourage teens to have fun, and provide condoms and abortions to spare them from living with the consequences of their actions. Besides, there is money to be made from providing birth control and abortion.

Liberals relate to the populace like parents with low expectations of their children. Studies abound that reveal children rise to the level of expectation, or conversely, sink to the level of low expectation.[2] Many parents and teachers have no idea of the power of their expectations, for good or for bad.

I remember in high school a fellow student who had visited the local university campus. He came back reporting how he had seen posters around the campus encouraging students to use birth control. It was 1968, and we knew only a couple of people in our high school who had actually had sex, so we were astonished that the state university expected sexual relationships between students. To us that was endorsement. A policy that was meant to help inadvertently harmed instead, by encouraging lower moral standards.

Moral Relativism

An outgrowth of being passion-oriented is that one's view of morality becomes self-serving. Pure liberals, consequently, have no moral anchor—values and ethical standards are relative to them. They regard the understanding of morality and virtue held by the Founding Fathers to be outdated and irrelevant. What is moral, they say, is determined by consensus—by how people live. Moral standards for liberals are like words in the dictionary—their meanings change and definitions are updated according to their usage in society. This means that for the liberal, morals are in a state of flux—what is immoral yesterday may be moral tomorrow. Their disregard for existing morals, in fact, will be what ushers in the change. For example, if enough people fornicate, eventually fornication will no longer be taboo, and unmarried couples will feel free to live together without embarrassment or shame. If enough people smoke marijuana, sooner or later Congress will drop it from a felony to a misdemeanor. If enough people break the law and trespass our borders, in time society will not penalize them, but will reward them with jobs, education for their children, and drivers' licenses. Hmmm…

Don't get me wrong. I'm not suggesting that liberals lack moral values. To the contrary—they have values and are passionate about them. It is because of their personal moral values that they believe every woman should have a right to abortion. It is their moral convictions that compel them to provide teens with prophylactic protection against STDs. And it is because of their commitment to decency that they fight for free expression—even when it means the right to be nude in public. Fifty years ago the moral values of liberals meant that most of them stood against abortion, condoms for teens, and public nudity. Liberals have moral values, but because they are a "progressive" people, their morals are subject to change. Most liberals disdain the label of "moral relativist," but that is exactly what "progressive" morals are.

This view of morality is frightening, because without an immutable moral standard, *expedience* becomes the rule. To elevate *expedience* means that whatever is thought best for the situation is what is deemed moral. Integrity and virtue, instead of acting as boundaries, become speed bumps, and are rolled over in pursuit of some higher good. Once morals are on a sliding scale, the end completely justifies the means. And if some, like the liberals, see themselves on the moral high ground, their consciences will permit them to do whatever they need to if they decide it is for everyone's ultimate best.

A liberal president, for example, might carry on an adulterous relationship in the White House, and have no qualms about lying under oath to cover it up. And when exposed, he will feel no shame nor be tempted to resign, because he believes that the good he offers the country outweighs his "mistakes." His supporters may acknowledge that adultery and lying are not good, but will mercifully overlook the indiscretions, because they, too, believe the country needs his liberal leadership. Their elevation of *expedience* over *integrity* is why they easily forgive the failures of liberal leaders, but have no tolerance for conservatives who fail. Besides, conservatives are the ones who claim to represent faith and values, while the liberals claim to represent free-spirited living. That means a conservative who falls is a hypocrite, but a liberal who falls was just careless. In their minds, the man who fails to live up to his own morals is worse than a man who makes no claim to have morals at all. The fact is, both should cause us concern.

When morality is arbitrary, society's standards get lower and lower. The scenario I just described occurred in 1998, just ten years after Gary Hart had been forced out of the 1988 presidential race for a comparatively minor scandal. Back then, the American people expected the president of the United States to have character. After all, it was reasoned, if a man lacks the character to keep his wedding vows to his wife, spoken before God and other witnesses, why should he be trusted to keep his oath of office? If a man would betray his own wife for personal pleasure, why would we expect him to be faithful to the American people? But because the liberal influence is so predominant in our society, in only one decade America's morals went from *"character wins our trust"* to *"character doesn't count."*

How absolutely insane!

In an effort to change society's values, those who grow up passion-driven instinctively seek to discard any societal morals that intrude on their "freedom." They take great offense at people who stand by traditional values. They do not want guilt, and with great anger they will silence anyone who makes them feel guilty. For example, someone can hold up a sign that says *"God Loves You"* and a liberal will condescendingly pat him on the head and say *"Isn't that nice for you."* But if someone holds up a sign that says *"Abortions Kill Children"* the liberal responds in rage. They do not mind if someone expresses, what to them, is an innocuous religious statement, but they do not want someone making them feel bad. I've seen it hundreds of times. Those who speak of traditional morals will be quickly accused of sitting in judgment, of hate speech, or of forcing their morality on others. It is interesting—those who push so strongly for tolerance and freedom of expression, and who want everyone else to embrace their ever-changing morals, will not tolerate anyone who expresses diffcrent opinions or values—even the values held by liberals in decades gone by. Hypocritical? Yes. Double standard? Absolutely, but they cannot see it. Remember—*they are blind*.

True Integrity

I have been using the words *virtue, character*, and *morality*, but I venture that most people these days, especially those under sixty, are uncertain of their meanings. Since these words were used by our nation's Founders to describe the traits necessary for our survival, it is critical that we understand them.

When our nation was founded, the world was somewhat of a barbaric place. Slavery was an accepted cultural practice; violence, murder, and public executions were commonplace. Gentlemen might fight a duel to the death over a simple insult.[3] Despite their "uncivilized" approach to life, throughout the American colonies and Europe there was a commonly held value of *personal honor*— our Founders called it *"sacred honor."*

Honor was held in such high regard that it was on par with a man's life and wealth. That is why it was such a testimony of sacrifice when our Founders pledged their lives, fortunes, and sacred honor to secure American independence. A man's honor was his reputation for integrity. If he could not be trusted, what value did he have in society? Even with the criminal types there was "honor among thieves." Can you envision a modern politician mouthing the words "I pledge my sacred honor"?

Personal honor played an important role in the Revolutionary War on both sides of the battle. With no military prisons in the colonies, the taking of prisoners created an interesting dilemma for both the colonial fighters and the British armies. After a battle, how did either side house the prisoners? History tells us that it was not uncommon that a captured soldier was offered a deal—if he promised he would not pick up a weapon and return to battle, he would be released to go back to his regiment. Those accepting the arrangement would give their word and be set free. Can you imagine what modern society would be like if people lived by such honesty and trustworthiness, or what Congress would be like if politicians could be trusted to only speak the truth?

A phrase occasionally heard in our culture, *"I would rather die than break a promise,"* came from the values of an era gone by. A person spoke such words and meant them when he or she wanted to testify of personal honor. Playwrights and writers of classic literature not uncommonly established the integrity of a character by having them speak a similar phrase.[4] Journalists used such phrases to describe the honor of those they wrote.[5] To a person of honor, death or personal harm was preferable to dishonesty.

Such integrity was what our Founders referred to when they used words such as *virtue* and *character*. Taken from Noah Webster's 1828 *American Dictionary*, the following definitions will help paint a more complete picture of good character that gives safe boundaries to *free expression*:

> VIRTUE: Moral goodness; the practice of moral duties and the abstaining from vice, or a conformity of life and conversation to the moral law. In this sense, virtue may be, and in many instances must be, distinguished from religion. The practice of moral duties merely from motives of convenience, or from compulsion, or from regard to reputation, is virtue, as distinct from religion. The practice of moral duties from sincere love to God and his laws, is virtue and religion. In this sense it is true, that virtue only makes our bliss below. Virtue is nothing but voluntary obedience to truth.

> VICE: In ethics, any voluntary action or course of conduct which deviates from the rules of moral rectitude, or from the plain rules of propriety; any moral unfitness of conduct, either from defect of duty, or from the transgression of known principles of rectitude. Vice differs from crime, in being less enormous. We never call murder or robbery a vice; but every act of intemperance, all falsehood, duplicity, deception, lewdness and the like, is a vice. The excessive indulgence of passions and appetites which in themselves are innocent, is a vice. The smoking of tobacco and the taking

of snuff, may in certain cases be innocent and even useful, but these practices may be carried to such an excess as to become vices. This word is also used to denote a habit of transgressing; as a life of vice. Vice is rarely a solitary invader; it usually brings with it a frightful train of followers.

INTEGRITY: The entire, unimpaired state of any thing, particularly of the mind; moral soundness or purity; incorruptness; uprightness; honesty. Integrity comprehends the whole moral character, but has a special reference to uprightness in mutual dealings, transfers of property, and agencies for others. The moral grandeur of independent integrity is the sublimest thing in nature, before which the pomp of eastern magnificence and the splendor of conquest are odious as well as perishable.

In understanding *virtue,* the key phrase to notice is "abstaining from vice," meaning unhealthy behavior which has the power to hold you in its grip. Essentially, to have virtue means to be free from habits, passions, or anything that might limit one's ability to make wise decisions or do what is right. The phrase the Founders used to describe virtue is one I have discussed at length—*self-government.*

Consider again the words of Thomas Jefferson:

Give up money, give up fame, give up science, give the earth itself and all it contains rather than do an immoral act. And never suppose that in any possible situation, or under any circumstances, it is best for you to do a dishonorable thing, however slightly so it may appear to you. Whenever you are to do a thing, though it can never be known but to yourself, ask yourself how you would act were all the world looking at you, and act accordingly. *Encourage all your virtuous dispositions, and exercise them whenever an opportunity arises, being assured that they will gain strength by exercise, as a limb of the body does, and that exercise will make them habitual. From the practice of the purest virtue, you may be assured you will derive the most sublime comforts in every moment of life, and in the moment of death.*[6]

Jefferson said, *"[A]sk yourself how you would act were all the world looking at you."* Character is not what we put on, but who we really are, which is evident when no one is there to watch. (Of course, this does not refer to flamboyant attention-seekers with no sense of shame, who might publicly perform any vulgar act for attention.)

For greater clarity, look at the phrase used by Noah Webster in his definition of virtue, *"Virtue is nothing but voluntary obedience to truth."* Virtue and good character mean we willingly choose to do what is right regardless of the consequences. Integrity, then, becomes an unchangeable standard and boundary—no matter how noble the goal, a person of character will not lie or steal to achieve it.

In the film *Chariots of Fire*, Eric Liddle, a runner in the 1924 Olympic Games, was under pressure from British officials to run a race scheduled for Sunday. Liddle refused, believing that to run on Sunday would dishonor God. While one British official complained that Liddle's priorities were off, putting God before country, another official noted that they should not expect to be able to persuade Liddle to violate his conscience—the drive and character that Liddle showed in standing by his convictions was the very trait that made him a great athlete. Liddle chose personal integrity and a clear conscience over the opportunity to run an Olympic race. The movie was a dramatized version of a true story, but that part of the film was historically accurate—Eric Liddle was a man whose integrity created inflexible boundaries for his behavior. His willingness to forego a lifetime opportunity for the sake of conscience epitomized the virtue spoken of by our nation's Founders.

Amazing Grace, another exceptional film, portrayed the story of statesman William Wilberforce (1759-1833), who led the fight to end the English slave trade. Known for his compassion, integrity, and tenacity, Wilberforce fought off physical afflictions and waged his abolition battle for more than forty years as a member of the House of Commons. He was resisted time and again, yet he refused to give up his campaign for human rights. The arguments he made against slavery were brilliant and his facts indisputable, yet he was resisted because his opponents had no interest in truth or in doing what was right—their minds were clouded by greed. The fact that Africans were self-determining humans, yet were being treated worse than animals, made no difference to these politicians—they couldn't even *begin* to consider the abolishment of slavery, because they feared the financial fallout. The film painted a classic picture of two kinds of people—those who stand for what is right, no matter what the outcome, and those who cannot see the obvious, because they are ruled by their passions.

I have personally witnessed a similar attitude only once in modern politics.

In 1993, Barbara Alby ran for district representative for the California State Assembly. I worked with her on her campaign and one day asked her, *"If you win, how do you plan to keep yourself from compromising your convictions like other conservatives we have helped get elected to office?"*

She answered me, *"If I win, I will go into office standing by my convictions, and if I am pressured to compromise, let them drum me out of the Assembly. Standing for what I believe in is more important than staying in power. If it comes to that I will gladly go down in flames."* Her words reflected the heart of integrity. She won the election, and in her terms of service she was better described as a *statesman* than as a *politician*, because she consistently valued integrity over political expedience.

Conservatives who have few convictions or are willing to compromise those they do have, are already liberal in their hearts. For professing conservatives to be truly conservative, the statements made by our Founding Fathers need to be true for them—they must be people free from the rule of their passions. They must resist the allure of power and the temptation of expedience. To be truly conservative, the *means* is just as important as the *end*. In fact, the end is not worth having if integrity is compromised to achieve it.

Redefining Virtue

As moral relativists, pure liberals' greatest struggle is that they view a utopian society as one void of traditional moral values. In fact, for them, anyone who promotes moral absolutes is self-serving and arrogant. They are offended by our Founding Fathers' stand for virtue. In order to justify themselves they either have to discredit our Founders or redefine virtue. They have done both.

Liberals, who dominate our schools and university faculties, present a view of history in which America's greatest heroes are oppressors, imperialists, and religious fanatics. In their skewed picture of history, Christopher Columbus, Captain John Smith, and the Pilgrims are evil. Under the influence of liberal-inspired political correctness, current history textbooks give extensive coverage to lesser historical figures, but comparatively little to those who founded our great country. Go to your local public school and check out an American history book for yourself. Or audit an American history course at your local university, where you will likely see a negative light cast upon our Founders. Men like George Washington, John Quincy Adams, Thomas Jefferson, Patrick Henry, and Benjamin Franklin are often portrayed as violent, overbearing slave owners and hypocrites who mishandled public funds. Or they are represented as heavy drinkers and philanderers—in other words, "normal" guys, whose ideas of virtue most certainly could not have included temperance and freedom from vice.

While some are on a rampage to denigrate our nation's Founders, most liberals simply redefine virtue. For them virtue is not about moral self-restraint—it is about *diversity* and selective *tolerance*. It is not about personal integrity—it is about standing against *discrimination* and about *giving to the deprived*. To liberals, the virtue spoken of by our Founders refers to their expressions of compassion. In the next few chapters we will examine the liberal view of compassion and demonstrate how it is a manifestation of indulgent parenting that, as we have discussed, is harmful to children and society.

CHAPTER SEVEN

COUNTERPRODUCTIVE LOVE

"What the vast majority of American children needs is to stop being pampered, stop being indulged, stop being chauffeured, stop being catered to. In the final analysis it is not what you do for your children but what you have taught them to do for themselves that will make them successful human beings."

— Ann Landers[1]

WHEN I WAS FOURTEEN, I decided I wanted to know the differences between the two major political perspectives, so I surveyed my grandfather, my parents, and my history teacher. Each gave a similar response. Liberals were concerned about the working man and helping the poor. Conservatives were concerned about making money and protecting big business. Liberals were progressive and looked to the future, while conservatives looked to the past and were stuck in their ways. Upon hearing those distinctions, there was no question for me— when I turned eighteen I would register and vote for liberals. I wanted to be hip and progressive, and certainly didn't want to be associated with rich people who only wanted to protect themselves and their own interests. I wanted to be identified with people that cared about people.

What I did not realize at the time was that the opposite was closer to the truth. Not only have I since discovered that the conservative approach to leadership shows more compassion than the liberal approach, but I have also found that individually, conservatives are exceedingly more generous to the needy than liberals.

Who Really Cares

In his book *Who Really Cares*, Professor Arthur Brooks presents the results of extensive research on the charitable giving patterns of conservatives and liberals. Professor Brooks used national surveys, tax returns, nonprofit reports, and interviews to gather his data, and the results were so shocking to him that he had to double-check his findings to be certain they were accurate. He discovered that annually, conservatives give to charitable causes about 30 percent more than liberals, and this despite conservatives having bigger families and, on the average, a 6 percent lower income. The difference is not a negligible 3 percent, but a whopping 30 percent—almost one-third more! The stereotype of selfish, rich conservatives is patently false.

Were the generosity simply reflected in monetary gifts, the difference could be attributed to the liberal belief that we give our tax dollars to the government, which in turn provides for the needy. However, Professor Brooks discovered that conservatives are not only more generous with their money, but they are 18 percent more likely to donate blood and consistently give more of their time as volunteers. According to Brooks: "If liberals and moderates gave blood at the same rate as conservatives, the blood supply of the United States would jump about 45 percent."[2] (With present trends, it is unfortunate that conservative values aren't passed on through blood transfusions.)

The findings of Professor Brooks bear out what I am contending—conservative ideals are rooted in genuine, heartfelt compassion. Liberals may have feelings of care and concern, but conservatives put their money where their mouth is.

Despite the facts, the false notion that liberals are the ones who care prevails. And there is a good reason for that. The social programs they support satisfy those they serve.

The problem with this, however, is that *satisfaction* does not accurately gauge if the *real* needs of people are being met. A lazy child is satisfied if you do for him that which he should do for himself; a greedy child is happy if you give him everything for which he asks; and a self-indulgent child is overjoyed when he is permitted to do whatever he wants, and does not have to live with the consequences of his actions. Such a child will "feel the love" and temporarily adore the one who indulges him. As I explained in Chapter Four, parents who live for their children's happiness may occasionally make them happy, but inadvertently rear them to be self-centered and irresponsible. It is possible for us to feel great affection for our children, and still harm them. Perhaps an experience I once had on a plane will help illustrate the point.

A couple of years ago I boarded a coast-to-coast flight to California. For the entire trip, I sat behind a couple and their four-year-old son. Watching them in that five-hour window of their lives is something I will never forget. The two parents were the most devoted Mommy and Daddy I have ever seen. I was amazed by the love and care they showed their little boy from departure to landing. At takeoff, when the seatbelt sign came on and the flight attendant would not permit the little guy to continue standing, Mommy and Daddy patiently explained as clearly as they could why the airline needed him to sit down and buckle his seatbelt. When, despite their efforts to reason with their four-year old, it was obvious that he was not going to grasp the importance of honoring FAA regulations, they tactfully distracted him with a new toy Daddy had saved for this moment. Mommy and Daddy outsmarted him with their distraction, and while he sat down to explore his new toy, they stealthily secured his seatbelt, and the plane was finally able to depart. They were so smooth he never knew he had been manipulated.

These parents were patient, kind, and attentive to their son's every want. In fact, they tried so hard to make him happy that I cannot remember seeing more conscientious parents. It was as if they lived only for him. Every request he had they met. Throughout the entire flight he was the center of their attention—providing for him movies, games, snacks, and toys. And when Junior insisted on visiting Grandma across the aisle, they immediately began pressuring passengers and flight attendants to make the change of seats possible. Their gracious and attentive manner towards their son reminded me of how servants might wait on royalty. In their realm, this boy was obviously king. They clearly loved him and wanted for him only good, but their love was counterproductive. To their credit, they were patient and kind, but they unknowingly were harming their son. As they made his happiness their *supreme* concern in life, his preoccupation with his own happiness grew as well. It was painful to see how demanding this overindulged child already was, and I could only imagine how self-absorbed he was going to become. It's just how human nature responds to indulgence. I've seen it so many times in my years of counseling.

These parents are like classic liberals in government. They have hearts full of love, and their actions show care and concern, but the ultimate effects are destructive to those they are trying to help.

Two Kinds of Liberals

I propose that there are two general classes of liberals—those in the *child role* and those in the *parent role*. Liberals in the *child role* are people in the general populace who want to be taken care of or demand the freedom to pursue their passions. They depend on liberals in the *parent role* to look after them and to protect their chosen lifestyles. They are generally demanding, impatient, and unthankful, and will attack anyone who tries to restrict their excesses or who expects them to exercise self-restraint. They have arrived at adulthood not much different than they were as kids— their "will-to-be-gratified" is still very much intact.

Those in the *parent role* are also still under the influence of their will-to-be-gratified, but they now serve as politicians, judges, attorneys, educators, journalists, and activists. They have the style of leadership that they gleaned from their parents, and erroneously think it is good to "coddle" those in the *child role*. So they try to provide for them whatever keeps them happy. Like overindulgent parents, whenever they hear the "children" complain, they seek to meet the need, thinking it is compassionate to rescue them from the consequences of their irresponsible actions. When the "children" feel they have been deprived, insulted, or hated, they raise their voices in shrill protest, and those in the *parent role* rush to their defense—consoling them with *"poor babies"* and attacking whichever conservative was responsible for the offense.

All this overindulgent care cultivates significant self-righteousness in the "parent." They feel noble, even superior for the devotion and care they have for the "children." In the liberal mind, conservatives are uncaring and heartless, while they as the "parents" are compassionate. They see themselves as the nation's "good guys"—all because they spoil the "children."

The relationship between the two classes of liberals is symbiotic—each feeds off the other and each justifies the other's existence. Those in the *child role* depend upon the "parent" to protect and provide for them. Those in the *parent role* crave the high self-worth they receive from feeling so caring for the "children." They enable each other—a classic case of *co-dependency*.

Liberals are not alone in this parent-child approach to politics. Enlightened conservatives also carry their parenting approach into government. However, because the conservative view of child rearing tends to foster self-control, self-reliance, and responsibility, conservative children typically grow up and take responsibility for themselves. They do not look to the government to take care of them or provide them unrestricted freedom to pursue their passions. When they become politicians, judges, attorneys, educators, journalists, and activists, they do not approach government from an overindulgent perspective, because they believe people are happiest and healthiest when they *work* for what they have. Of course, liberals in the *child role* expect to be coddled, so they despise the conservative efforts to help them take responsibility for themselves.

The Harm of Overindulgent Love

America, as a society, is unique among nations. We are the most benevolent, each year giving to the needy, both internationally and domestically, close to the sum total of the entire rest of the world.[3] And why shouldn't we have such a generous outlook—we were founded on principles of biblical morality and compassion.

Although many have forsaken the morals of our Founders, most have maintained the philanthropic ideals. Help for the needy is an integral part of our American worldview. Our loss of morals, however, is responsible in part for convoluting our understanding of care for the needy. True help should promote personal responsibility while providing temporary assistance, but ours has become overindulgent love.

If you recall from our discussion of proper parenting in Chapter Four, when children are overindulged they develop an exalted sense of their own importance. Self-centeredness grows, and they cultivate a perspective of entitlement, thinking that what they desire is *owed* to them. This high sense of self-worth develops in them a lack of appreciation, causing them to become demanding of what they have come to think are their *rights*. They carry this self-centered outlook into their adult life—in both the *parent role* and the *child role*.

If you have had any dealings with the homeless, perhaps you have noticed that many of them think free food, housing, and medical care is *owed* to them. If you know anyone addicted to illegal drugs you may have heard the opinion that the government owes them clean needles or free methadone treatment. If you have listened to those who are promiscuous perhaps you have heard them demand more funding to find a cure for deadly STDs like AIDS. It is no surprise that children, whose indulgent parents cleaned up their messes, have grown up to believe that someone else is obligated to help them clean up the mess they have made of their lives. It is also no surprise that children raised by parents with an entitlement mentality arrive at adulthood with the same unhealthy outlook.

Homelessness

As a pastor for many years I have had a great deal of contact with the homeless. I have spent time on the streets handing out food and blankets. There have been rainy seasons in which I had homeless people sleeping in my home or living at the church office. We have brought them to our farm to teach them how to work and to help them break their addictions. I have given them jobs and helped them manage their free monthly government subsidies. All this I share simply to demonstrate that the comments I make are not merely philosophical or speculative—they have been born from my personal experience.

As a young man, I first began reaching out to the homeless with great enthusiasm. I remember the joy I felt the first time I handed out free blankets on the streets of Sacramento. The enthusiasm started to wane a year later, however, when I realized that those we helped rarely appreciated that they had received something for nothing. I vividly recall one Thanksgiving when I was passing out turkey dinners to the hundreds of homeless who had gathered at a park for the event. Person after person expressed discontent with what they received. One complained because the turkey was no longer hot, another was upset that he didn't get a napkin, and another said he felt "ripped off" because others had received cinnamon rolls and he only had a biscuit. Many said, "Thank you," but just as many expressed discontentment. That day I found myself questioning how to best help those in humble circumstances who lacked humility.

At that time my mother was president of the board for a well-known homeless shelter in her city, so I called and told her about the demanding attitudes and lack of appreciation I was witnessing. Her response opened my eyes. She explained that the people we had been helping were probably not homeless at all—they were *"street people"*—in other words, *transients, bums,* and *hobos.* They did have a home—it was the *streets,* which they had chosen in order to allow themselves an irresponsible lifestyle. She went on to explain that a truly homeless person was typically a responsible individual who was temporarily without a place to live. It was her experience that most genuinely homeless people would be too embarrassed to show up for a public event like the ones we staged at the park. To qualify to stay in the homeless shelter she oversaw, there were two requirements: People must show no sign of substance abuse and had to prove that they were looking for work. The kind we attracted to our free giveaways were not truly "homeless" and would not even qualify to stay in her homeless shelter.

My mother's words made great sense to me. They helped me better understand news accounts involving the homeless. I was a radio talk show host at the time and had covered the story of a business owner who had wandered through downtown Sacramento offering jobs to the hundreds of "homeless" he met on the streets. He gave up after a couple of days because he could find no workers—only excuses. They all were interested in the money, but none was willing to forego their simple lifestyle void of commitments and responsibility. In that season there was also the account of "homeless" people going into the capital building to pound on Governor Deukmejian's door to make demands. By the time that story came out I understood the difference between the humble homeless and insolent street people, and it still blew my mind! How did lazy, irresponsible people ever get the idea that they were owed something they had not earned? Where did such presumption come from? It may be inherent to human nature, but it was likely exacerbated by indulgent parents or by liberal leaders in the *parent role* who had been providing for them.

I read an anecdote in *Reader's Digest* years ago that beautifully illustrates my point. A woman told the story of how she was stopped on the street one day by a beggar who asked for money. She fished in her purse for loose change and took a while to find some. In fact, it was taking her so long, the beggar impatiently complained, *"Come on, Lady. I don't have all day."*

Until we start distinguishing between homeless and hobos, and focus on helping those who are ready to take responsibility for themselves, our overindulgent approach to government will only reward laziness and foster greater irresponsibility in our citizens. Under our present indulgent approach, those we call "homeless" lack any motivation to take responsibility for themselves and improve their lives. After all, why should they even think about working when we have taught them it comes for free? All they have to do is look pitiful or squawk loud enough. If the government or overindulgent religious groups do not provide for them, they just have to hold a sign "WILL WORK FOR FOOD" and softhearted members of the community will enable them with their loose change.[4]

The Disadvantaged

The homeless are not the only souls who qualify for government handouts. Unwed teenage mothers, people with disabilities (including adults with ADD and drug addiction), and some minorities are eligible for help with education, childcare, job opportunities, and housing benefits. I don't want to suggest that all of these people are irresponsible and undeserving of help. What I want to communicate is that it is *indiscriminate* help that is dangerous, because it fosters laziness and an entitlement mentality.[5]

An unwed mother we were counseling many years ago was a classic case of entitlement thinking. This young lady lived in a government-subsidized house in a nice neighborhood, was given enough welfare to live on, and received free medical care for her and her child. We happened to be visiting her one day when she checked her mailbox and discovered that her welfare check had not arrived according to schedule. It had been a holiday weekend, so the check would apparently be delayed a day. The young lady was furious, and vowed she would go down to the welfare office and give them a piece of her mind. After all, she had bills to pay, and she needed her money *now*!

To calm her down my wife tried to reason with her, reminding her that she had done nothing to earn her checks, and that she should be thankful for the government's gift, no matter what day it arrived. It didn't work. She had become so accustomed to receiving the gift of taxpayers' money that she had come to believe she actually had a *right* to it. In her mind the money was not the taxpayers' or the government's—it was *hers*. She was convinced she deserved it because she had a hard lot in life.

Did you follow that? She believed she deserved compensation because she had a tough life!

A friend of mine found the same problem when he went to Mexico to start a community outreach in a small town in Baja. He set up a resource center from which he dispensed free food, clothes, and other items to the needy. After a few months he discovered that not only were those he helped no longer appreciative of his gifts, but they had come to *expect* ALL their needs to be met for free. The

73

significance of the change finally hit him one day when he loaded his truck with food and returned to an encampment of migrant farm workers. After he parked, the people began to gather, but did not wait their turns to receive their gifts—they stormed the truck and started grabbing everything they could.

He had gone to Mexico with noble dreams, but this response he never saw coming—the more he gave them, the lazier, more dependent, and demanding they became. He had become their American "sugar daddy." It didn't take him long to figure out that his indulgent approach fostered an entitlement mindset and was doing the people more harm than good. He found that by turning his resource center into a thrift shop where items could be bought for pennies, the people had their needs met, but gained a greater sense of personal responsibility.

The Haves and the Have-Nots

I have found that a presumptive attitude is common among indulged people. They come to believe that those with jobs, money, or homes are the "haves" and those without are the "have-nots." In their minds, since the *haves* are "lucky" enough to have so much, they are obligated to share it with the *have-nots*, who are just "down on their luck." It has been my experience that these people literally believe help is *owed* to them as if it were a paycheck they had earned. In their minds it is not about personal responsibility—it is about luck—those with good luck owe help to those with bad luck.

As a fulltime pastor for many years I regularly received calls at the church office from strangers asking for money, food, or clothes. Some had legitimate needs, but most were scammers. We were more than willing to assist those with genuine needs, but would never help the ones who acted as if we owed them something, particularly if they tried to manipulate us with guilt. Guilt is an effective tool in the hands of those who know how to use it, but it is most effective on the *haves* who forget that it was not *good luck* that gave them what they have, but *hard work*.

What so many seem to forget is that the vast majority of *haves* only *have* because they labored for it. Many people who consider themselves the *have-nots* are *without,* because they have been irresponsible and are reaping what they have sown. Had they worked harder in school, chosen better friends, steered clear of premarital sexual activities, stayed out of gangs, been more diligent at work, or avoided drugs and alcohol they would not have brought on themselves so many hardships. Rather than feel sorry for themselves for having such "bad luck" or for growing up with so little, they should hold themselves responsible for how they responded to life's challenges. It is that shirking of personal responsibility that forms the basis for entitlement thinking.

Some might think that those who were born into low-income families are not reaping what they sowed—they have less, because they started out life with less. That line of thinking is deeply flawed—it presumes that a low income inhibits the growth of good character and a hard-work ethic, thereby determining one's level of success in life. In fact, neither a lack of money nor a surplus has anything to do with who a person becomes, particularly in America. Who we become and what we achieve is determined by how we respond to life's challenges. Think about it—in every position of influence in both business and government are people who were born and raised in poverty!

Abraham Lincoln was born into poverty, had little formal education, failed in business twice, and lost six major elections, yet persisted and won our nation's top office. Andrew Johnson spent his childhood in poverty yet went on to become the seventeenth president of the United States. Justice Clarence Thomas grew up poor, in a housing project void of a sewage system and paved roads, yet graduated from Yale Law School and earned a seat on the Supreme Court. Bill Cosby's family lived without much money while he was growing up, but he went on to earn a doctorate from the University of Massachusetts. George Washington Carver faced the challenges of poverty, slavery, and being orphaned, yet became one of our nation's premier inventors. Dwight Eisenhower, while not growing up in poverty, overcame a life of incredible hardships to become a West Point graduate, five-star general, and our thirty-fourth president.

We must reject the fallacy that low income is only a curse and an insurmountable obstacle to success. The truth is that its challenges lay a path to developing character, which paves the way to success. Well-equipped parents can set an example and train their children how to walk that path.

Socialism

Perhaps by this point some have noticed that woven into the fabric of overindulgent love are elements of *socialistic* thinking. Indulgent parents commonly want to keep all things *equal* between children, because they don't want anyone feeling deprived or upset. They dread the words, *"It's not fair!"* If Billy has been invited out to a movie with his friends, Mommy is concerned that little sister Mary feels left out, so she takes her to a movie, too. If neighbor Joey saves up his money and buys himself a new baseball glove, Billy pressures Daddy into buying him a new glove. And when Mom and Dad hear that "absolutely everyone" at school is getting a limo for the senior prom, they figure their child needs one as well.

Liberals in the *parent role* do the same in society. They have listened to those in the *child role* cry "UNFAIR" when they lack what others have, and they do the only loving thing they can do—they push for equal opportunity, welfare, and socialized programs to insure that everything is equal. For things to be "fair," and the poor and disadvantaged to be happy, they must be given things others have had to earn. In the liberal mind they have a *right* to the advantages earned by the successful. To be without them is to be *deprived*.

Life Is Hard

One of the reasons that we as Americans, both liberals and professing conservatives alike, tend to overindulge our children is that *we* enjoy so much affluence and indulge *ourselves* so much. We are preoccupied with a soft life and seek to avoid most inconvenience and discomfort. Product developers realize this and design their products and services to appeal to our desire for ease and simplicity. That is why so many electronic devices have remote controls these days. It's also one reason everything from roller skates to cars, cell phones, and computers are improved every year—Americans want everything slicker, faster, and easier. Are they making crayons yet with a built-in camera? NO? Just wait.

We have become so accustomed to luxury that we think real suffering is a slow Internet connection or having to wait in line at the Department of Motor Vehicles. We think we suffer when we run out of our favorite brand of toilet paper, when the air conditioning in our car breaks down, or when we get stuck on a one-lane highway behind an overly cautious driver. For some, hunting for the TV remote is one of the greatest causes of grief in their day. Most of us are so soft that we simply could not imagine living at a time in history when there was no indoor plumbing and toilets were just holes in the ground. In all our affluence and ease, most of us have little tolerance for suffering.

I was in Uganda a few years ago at a mission compound in the bush teaching community leaders about effective parenting and healthy family life. When I wasn't teaching I was able to visit the people in the community. Those I met lived in mud huts. They had no electricity, and most of them had to get their water from a source at least a mile away. The water had to be carried in five-gallon containers, and because it was undrinkable, it had to be boiled over a campfire.

Although the people lived in mud huts, they were meticulously clean. They swept the dried mud floors of their huts and kept the grounds around them free from trash and clutter. These were not the most impoverished people in the world, but they were the poorest I had ever seen. To make a living, entire families dug up clay to fashion into bricks and sell. Others spent their days smashing rocks with hammers to create gravel, which they sold to construction workers.

One afternoon I came upon a boy, who could not have been more than five years old, digging for clay in a deep hole all by himself. He was joyful and content—obviously having learned at an early age that hard work was part of life. As I watched him dig I tried to imagine an average American child in this hot, sticky climate, digging clay unsupervised or hammering out gravel with his family. The picture in my mind was not pretty. Most families here have spoiled their children, raising them to think that their comfort is supreme. Were such families injected into the Ugandan lifestyle, both parents and children would be in for a rude awakening. I cannot help but wonder how long it would take before such a lifestyle would transform that family.

What stood out to me about the Ugandans was that by American standards they lived in deprivation, but none of them seemed to know it. I met no one who thought their lifestyle was suffering. To them, life was hard, and that was life, but it had nothing to do with their emotional disposition. They were not sad or miserable—just the opposite, they were the happiest people I have ever met in the world.[6] As I think about it, the unhappiest people I have met are from affluent countries. I am willing to bet that you can guess why that would be.

The example of life in Uganda stands in stark contrast to the hardships we whine about in America. Yes, divorce, disease, and death for any person in any culture is hard, but I am speaking about our daily expectations for life. Too few of us know how to endure hardships, and so we fail to cultivate emotional resilience. We think we *suffer* when we are simply deprived of ease or luxury.

An aversion to pain is only human, but in America we have developed an incredibly low threshold for any kind of discomfort. This has made us intolerant of the daily suffering in life that could develop character and emotional strength. It has caused us to rescue our children from the hardships that cultivate personal responsibility and foster maturity. Instead, we tune our ears to their whining and rescue them from the adversity that should be preparing them for the challenges they will face in their adult lives.

For too many parents, love for their children is counterproductive. They care so much about them that they try to protect them from all the pain of life. But in doing so, they deprive them of key opportunities for growth. If children are to persevere with contentment through the hardships they will undoubtedly face as grownups, they must be taught when young that they can handle the suffering of picking up their toys or eating spinach.

Sylvester Stallone illustrated one aspect of this principle in a deleted scene from the 2006 movie *Rocky Balboa*. In this scene, Rocky says that when he was young he would *"be squeezing a ball until I felt my hand was gonna explode. I was teaching myself to be uncomfortable, cuz I knew being uncomfortable might come in handy some day."* In a film that few people would watch to glean lessons of wisdom, Rocky reinforces the profound truth that learning to handle discomfort when young is preparation for the challenges of real life.

Over the last several decades, because fewer children have been raised to thrive in discomfort, America has grown progressively softer. According to military officials new recruits lack the level of personal discipline of those in prior generations. In the course of a massive study of inductees from 1996 to 1998[7] researchers made the following observation: *"New recruits were frequently characterized as lazy, selfish, out of shape, undisciplined, lacking in morals, challenging every order or decision or rule, having no respect for authority...and unwilling to shift from an individual mentality to a team orientation."*[8] What else should we expect? We live in an age when children are indulged and grow up less prepared for the hardships of life. They lack the discipline needed by those entering military service.

Disappointment, rejection of peers, monotony of chores, and the grief of losing a soccer game are all aspects of adversity from which we must not continually rescue our children. It takes selfless love for parents to ignore their own overly protective feelings and not cave in to children's whining, sulking, or tears. Our children must learn from us that hard things in life can be faced and overcome, and that contentment need not depend upon having one's own way in life. Until they do, they will not be truly happy.

Indulgence and Happiness

Parents who give supremacy to their children's happiness tend *not* to raise happy children. Even liberal author Betty Friedan acknowledges, *"Strange new problems are being reported in the growing generations of children whose mothers were always there, driving*

79

them around, helping them with their homework—an inability to endure pain or discipline or pursue any self-sustained goal of any sort, a devastating boredom with life."[9]

Indulgence fosters such an elevated view of self that dissatisfaction becomes the norm, expressing itself through constant grumbling and complaining. Parents find that such children grow up with high expectations of satisfaction, but happiness for them is usually elusive. As I mentioned earlier, the happiest and most secure children are those whose parents do not pander to their whims, but show their tender love along with directive leadership, consistency, and firm rules. Happiness is a common by-product of well-trained character—in the words of Thomas Jefferson, *"without virtue, happiness cannot be."*[10]

When indulged children reach adulthood and become politically active, it is no surprise that they are rarely content. When they are not in power they are angry with the conservatives who are in power. And when they *are* in power they are always angry with the conservatives who disagree with them or their policies. They blame their constant anger on conservatives, whose policies lack what they think is compassion. But their dissatisfaction can generally be traced back to the outlook on life they cultivated in childhood.

Research supports my assertion. Conservatives tend to be happier in life than both liberals and independents. According to a series of Gallup polls over the years, Republicans consistently rate happier than Democrats—as much as 12 percent higher, even when liberals are in power.[11] Republicans also feel significantly better about their mental health than Democrats, with 58 percent rating it as *excellent*, compared with only 38 percent of Democrats.[12] It only follows that conservatives are happier in the area of sex and romance. In 2004, after one of the most comprehensive sex surveys in decades, the ABC News polling unit found that on average, Republicans rate their sexual happiness 9 to 10 percent higher than Democrats.[13]

I am convinced that if conservatives can rid their parenting of liberal tendencies, the percentage of differences will increase in the next generation. If we continue to indiscriminately rescue the needy in society from all the consequences of their choices the way we tend to overprotect our children, America will never escape the welfare state we have become, and we shall continue to see our families disintegrate and the crime rate grow. Liberals must learn the harm they cause by their indulgent love. Sadly, they tend to be totally unaware of this, because it is the framework through which they view life.[14]

CHAPTER EIGHT

RESCUING VICTIMS

"A Peanuts cartoon showed Peppermint Patty talking to Charlie Brown. 'Guess what, Chuck,' she said. 'The first day of school, and I got sent to the principal's office. It was your fault, Chuck.' 'My fault?' He sputtered. 'How could it be my fault? Why do you say everything is my fault?' 'You're my friend, aren't you, Chuck?...You should have been a better influence on me.'"[1]

IN COMPARISON to the rest of the world, America is a nation of great compassion. We provide for the needy and we rescue victims of calamity and injustice, whether they are our own citizens or those of another country. After the tsunami struck the coast of Southeast Asia in 2004, American individuals and private citizen groups gave more than $200 million towards relief before our government responded with its own $350 million aid package.[2] Total charitable giving for that year from individuals and private organizations was more than $283 billion. In 2006, giving to charitable causes increased, totaling almost $300 billion.[3] American citizens lead the world in generosity and care for victims.

Most of our giving, and a significant portion of our tax dollars, fund "compassion" programs here at home. We provide safe havens for women escaping domestic violence, our schools provide free meals for malnourished children, and shelters abound for the homeless. We offer Medicare, food stamps, and subsidized housing for the financially disadvantaged. Our nation has tens of thousands of programs to rescue victims. However, there is a problem. Liberals have lost the ability to distinguish between true victims and those who suffer as a result of their own irresponsibility. True victims deserve our compassion, but it is not compassionate to habitually rescue or reward those who are irresponsible. Parents who coddle in this way may see their children remain dependent, self-centered, and thankless well into adulthood. Governments who do this produce the same results with their citizens. Such "compassion" is not truly loving when it promotes behavior that is destructive to any society.

As I illustrated in Chapter Seven, loving parents can take their protective role too far and rescue their children from the challenges of life that pave the way to maturity. To lay a framework for discussing these concepts let's look again at Point 5 of Chapter Four:

> Parental love compels us to nurture and care for our children—and to protect them from all suffering. The problem is that misapplied love can be harmful to our children's development. When we continually rescue them from having to suffer the consequences of their actions we keep them from developing a proper sense of personal responsibility. We accidentally foster immaturity by doing for our children that which they are able and need to do for themselves.

Responsible people are not only reliable, they do not depend on others to clean up their messes or pay for their obligations. When our children make a mess they must be required to clean it up. When they break something they need to repair or replace it. Restoration and restitution are key expressions of personal responsibility.

If our child leaves his bike out in the front yard, despite our warnings, and it is stolen, we must not run off and buy him another one. Children will learn responsibility by having to save their money to buy another one themselves. If they damage a toy belonging to a friend, they must buy a new one whether asked to or not. Parental defensiveness at these times feels so right, but is damaging to our children. From the time they are young we must reinforce to them that it is their duty to clean up their own messes, repair what they damage, and pay their own bills, including their own parking tickets and traffic fines.

If we do not hold our children accountable for themselves, but rescue them from the consequences of their actions, they grow up to believe that pursuit of personal pleasure without consequence is their supreme right. They develop a "victim" mentality, thinking that they are not responsible for the circumstances that they have brought upon themselves. In fact, they become convinced that someone else is to blame for their distress, and thus it becomes someone else's duty to take care of their problems.

In addition, parents inadvertently teach children irresponsibility by issuing too many warnings or by reinforcing bad behavior. When a child is caught sneaking dessert before dinner, parents encourage bad behavior by merely admonishing him not to do it again, and allowing him to finish eating what he took. That is no different than teachers who consistently permit students to turn in assignments past the due date, without penalty. Consistently allowing children to behave irresponsibly without consequence encourages future misconduct. In fact, such leniency cultivates the perspective that mercy is *owed* them.

Yes, parents are the protectors of their children, but to grow into maturity, our children must not be rescued from every challenge they face, especially if the challenges have resulted from their choices. They will develop a "victim" mentality and continue to hold others responsible for all the negative fallout in their lives. They will fail to develop the third key element of maturity— *personal responsibility.*

Let's look again at why personal responsibility is an essential quality in a good citizen:

> A responsible person is one who accepts personal accountability for his own actions. He does not make excuses or blame others for his failures, and does not expect others to make up for his mistakes. He takes responsibility for himself and pays his own bills in life.... When a child is not held responsible to fulfill his personal duties, but is cut slack time and again, he grows up thinking that...he should not have to live with the consequences of his actions, and

comes to develop a "victim" mentality—nothing is ever his
fault—someone else is always to blame for his misery.

Perhaps it would be good at this point to define what I mean by
"victim" mentality. To understand this we must distinguish between
true and false victims, or better yet—*full* victims and *semi* victims.

A *full* victim is a passive recipient of harm. It is one who
contributed nothing to his affliction and lacked any capacity to
control its effects. Full victims are *innocent*. In this category are
people who have suffered child abuse, domestic violence, rape,
or other kinds of criminal assault. It includes those who are
genetically predisposed to a disease, victims of drunk drivers,
and children who contracted AIDS in utero. Few will dispute that
these people and others like them are true victims and deserve
our utmost care and mercy.

Semi victims are those who may suffer a mishap or incur a
condition, but are not innocent—they have contributed in some
way to their affliction. Included in this category are smokers with
lung cancer, athletes injured in sports, and prostitutes with STDs.
It also includes incarcerated criminals, sexually active teenage
mothers, and street people, not to mention lazy students who
earn low grades, sugar-eaters with cavities, and bullies who lose
fights. They still deserve our compassion and care, but in some
way they are victims of their own choices and are reaping what
they have sown.

Many people we have come to regard as victims are not *full*
victims at all—they are *semi* victims. We mislabel transients and
vagrants as "homeless," and treat them as if they are victims of
poverty, when in fact they are usually perpetrators of laziness who
are reaping the fruit of their irresponsibility. We tend to view unwed
teenage mothers as unfortunate victims of circumstances, but they
are, most often, sexually active individuals who conceive children as
a consequence of their choices. Welfare recipients are commonly
treated as helpless victims of poverty who cannot rise above their
disadvantaged upbringing, but many are individuals who have not
taken full responsibility for themselves. If American society is to be
helped, conservatives must identify and forsake liberal "victim"
thinking—both in their parenting and in their governing.

The Victim Mentality

It is the *semi* victim who most often develops a "victim" mentality. This mentality is illustrated by the following three perspectives:

"You're responsible for the problems I have brought upon myself."

"You're responsible to rescue me from my hardships."

"You're responsible for how I respond to you."

"You're responsible for the problems I have brought upon myself."

People with a victim mentality overlook the fact that they contributed to their condition. In their minds someone or something else is liable for what they have done. They have lots of excuses, and their explanations lift the burden of guilt. This shifting of responsibility means they may blame the innocent for problems they have brought upon themselves. And if the "victim" has been *forced* to reap the consequences of their foolishness or misdeeds, they will blame the one who reports them or executes justice.

Rejection of personal responsibility is rampant in our country. Perhaps some of you will remember the news account in 1992 of a Chicago schoolteacher who had lost his job for habitual tardiness. He sued the school district to get his job back, claiming he was afflicted with "chronic lateness syndrome." Rather than learn a lesson and change his ways, he blamed the district for intolerance of his "disability." Mayor Marion Barry of Washington, D.C., was filmed smoking crack cocaine, but instead of owning up and taking his licks, he blamed law enforcement, claiming he was a victim of racism. An FBI agent embezzled $2,000 from the government and lost it gambling at a casino. He was fired for the theft, but successfully sued to regain his job. He convinced the court that his compulsion to steal money to support his gambling habit was a "handicap" and, therefore, he was entitled to special treatment under federal laws forbidding discrimination against the handicapped. The government had to give him his job back and pay for treatment of his "disability."

It seems we live in an age when it never hurts to try blaming someone or something else for what you have done wrong.

I once spoke with a man who had recently been arrested for drug dealing. He told me the police had pulled him over in his truck and discovered a large quantity of drugs in his glove compartment. He admitted to me that the drugs were his, but he owned no responsibility for his arrest. He blamed the police for stopping him without just cause. In his mind, if he was going to jail, it was the fault of the police for violating proper procedure. He was confident he had played the game right, and provided the police with no reason to stop him. Therefore, he shouldn't have been stopped, they shouldn't have looked in his glove box, and he shouldn't be going to jail. He felt certain he was a victim of injustice.

Tragically, this man's common-law wife was already serving time for drug-related charges, and now he was likely going to leave his children without parents, yet he accepted no responsibility. He was about to lose his freedom and his children, and he sincerely believed that it was not because of his foolish choices, but because he was a victim. In his deluded mind he believed it was the legal system that was destroying his family!

A couple of years earlier, this man's forty-year-old neighbor had been sent to jail for the third time on drug-related charges. He was found guilty of manufacturing methamphetamine in his barn despite his claim that he was merely in possession of household chemicals. This repeat drug offender's sixty-five-year-old father disregarded the overwhelming evidence, and blamed the police for his son's arrest. He believed his son's excuses that he was merely mixing household chemicals. This was a classic case of a parent who had helped cultivate a victim mentality in his child and continued to reinforce it well into his adult years.

Disavowing personal responsibility and shifting blame is innate to humans. In the UK a man with dyslexia and dyscalculia is suing his bank for not accommodating his disabilities. He is unable to comprehend mathematics and figures in written form, so he cannot understand his bank statement, which he claims has cost him a bad credit rating and thousands of dollars in overdraft charges. Rather than assume responsibility for himself and find an acquaintance to help him read his bank statements, or give his business to an institution that provides the services he desires, he believes it is his bank's duty to provide someone trained in his disabilities to help him each month.[4]

Avoiding Consequences

While doing research for this book I worked as a substitute high school teacher, and was astonished by what I experienced — students were shocked when I sent them to the principal's office after just one classroom misdeed. Apparently they were used to being warned multiple times, so often, in fact, that they failed to understand simple justice. Their perception was that they should not be held responsible until they had been warned sufficiently and given a few more chances, rather than receiving just one warning at the beginning of the class period. They saw my requirements that they not chat among themselves and that they raise their hand to secure permission before speaking as an unreasonable standard. They were like many in our culture who feel like victims of injustice when someone simply holds them accountable for breaking a rule or violating a law.

When children grow up with no grasp of basic justice and without an understanding of personal responsibility, should we be surprised that our culture is dominated by "victims" who blame everyone and everything else for their behavior, attitudes, reactions, and problems? And when society's leaders in the "parent role" oversee the country in the same manner in which they oversee their children, is it any surprise that so much legislation is designated to the special treatment of "victims"?

"You're responsible to rescue me from my hardships."

Victims think they shouldn't have to live with the consequences of their actions. And because they hold others responsible for the afflictions they bring upon themselves, they think it is someone else's duty to rescue them. In their minds, they are entitled. At the least, they believe their condition, or the afflictions suffered by their ancestors, earns them special treatment. I have observed that even full victims can be so deluded by self-pity that they develop the perspective that "everybody owes me."

"You pay for my mistake."

Many years ago I hired a man to come to my house and trim my trees for $300. He insisted he was very experienced and knew how to protect my house and shrubbery from falling branches. He did a fine job, but at one point allowed a cut branch to fall from a tree and destroy a section of rain gutter at the corner of my house. Before he had finished the job I was able to call a gutter repairman, and get an estimate over the phone for replacing the damaged section—$125.

When the tree trimmer finished up and presented me with his bill for $300, I presented him with mine for gutter repairs. He was stunned and angry—he didn't think it was his responsibility to pay for the damage he had caused. He thought I should pay for his tree trimming work, plus the cost of rectifying his mistake. I told him I would pay him $175 now and the additional $125 when he had the gutter repaired. He insisted that he knew no one who could do it for him. He was absolutely flabbergasted that I expected him to fix or pay for what he had broken.

It was obvious he had not been raised to be accountable for himself. I felt badly for him—he literally could not grasp that it was his duty to pay for what he had done. He took his $175 and drove away. I waited a few weeks to see if he was going to return and take care of the repairs. Finally, when he didn't return, I spent $125 on gutter repairs.

I assume most people would have done as I did, but some might have felt sorry for him and caved in to reward his irresponsibility. That would have been bad for him and bad for society—he would have missed the opportunity to learn personal responsibility. It's too bad he didn't acknowledge his responsibility and humbly accept the repair. If he had demonstrated himself to be a man of integrity, I would have canceled his debt. As it was, his "victim" perspective led him to believe that someone else should pay for his mistake, which insured that *he* would have to.

"You're to blame for the spread of a deadly STD."

In 1989, I participated in a pro-life rally on the steps of the California state capital. As expected at such an event, there were abortion advocates protesting against our rally for children. Among the abortion supporters were some whose concern did not appear to be the issue of abortion, but rather AIDS research. One young man walked the circumference of the pro-life crowd repeating the same slogan for more than an hour. He shouted a challenge, *"Seventeen thousand dead from AIDS. Where were you? Seventeen thousand dead from AIDS. Where were you?"*

He obviously wasn't blaming us for committing the acts that spread the disease—he was inferring that the ones who did commit the deeds and contracted the virus would not have suffered its effects if the government had spent more money to find a cure. To him it wasn't the drug users or the licentious that were to blame for their own sickness—everyone who failed to rescue them was at fault. In his mind, promiscuous people should be able to pursue their passions without having to endure any natural consequences—thoughts typical of an overindulged child who grew up without learning self-restraint, and personal responsibility.

Please understand that I do not take lightly any man's death. Whether it was seventeen thousand who died or just seventeen, their deaths were tragedies. As a pastor I have been with many people on their deathbeds and officiated at numerous funerals. Some have died as innocent victims of diseases or accidents, while some were not innocent, but contributed to their own deaths—they made the foolish choices of chain smoking, drinking to excess, or engaging in risky activities. Whether people die innocently or because they choose to take chances with their own lives, there is always pain for the loved ones left behind, not to mention the hole they leave in society. I am always grieved.

In the case of AIDS, there is no question that the vast majority of Americans who have contracted HIV could have avoided the disease if they had not given themselves over to their passions time after time. Illegal drug use and promiscuity, whether in heterosexual or homosexual relationships, are risky behaviors, and the choice to take those risks is playing "AIDS roulette." Those who choose to play take such chances because they are driven by their passions and can no longer think clearly. It makes no objective sense to continually place one's life on the line for the sake of momentary gratification. I realize that skydivers risk their lives for the adrenaline rush they receive from jumping out of airplanes, but no one blames the government if their chutes fail to open.

It is irrational thinking when people in a high-risk lifestyle expect taxpayers to subsidize their lack of self-restraint. With that mentality, rock climbers could band together and demand that the government erect nets at the bottom of all mountains to reduce their risk. The rationale is exactly the same.

The bottom line is that people who choose to live a risky life should be willing to suffer the consequences. The harm they bring upon themselves is their own fault—not the fault of those who choose to live more safely. If people who have chosen to live safely come to the rescue of the risk-takers, they are doing them a favor—it is not their obligation. By no means should those who live dangerously think it is anyone's duty to rescue them. And in no way should those who don't come to the rescue feel guilty for not doing them the favor. A favor is always an undeserved gift.

People in the *child role* think others are responsible for the problems their behavior creates, and liberals in the *parent role* think it is loving to rescue them. It is better for society's members to develop the virtue of self-restraint than to be encouraged in the behavior that our founders warned would destroy our moral fiber and, ultimately, our nation.

"You're responsible for how I respond to you."

The concept of "victimization" is based on the idea that I am not in control of myself—that who I am and how I respond is determined by someone or something else. I am at the mercy of people and things that influence me. I will, therefore, hold them responsible for the reaction evoked in me.

This element of "victim" thinking is deeply rooted in all of us, and might manifest throughout our day. Consider the "victim" elements of the following phrases: *"See what you made me do?!" "Can't you see what you're doing to me?!" "I wouldn't have done what I did if you hadn't done what you did to me!"* Yes, I realize that those phrases might be uttered by innocent victims who had no choice in their response. But more often than not, we speak them when we want to blame someone else for our reaction.

Think about it—is a man who resents his wife's coldness justified in his adultery; is a man excused for hitting his mother because he felt he couldn't handle her nagging; or is a neighbor justified in attacking your children for playing on his lawn? I assume you would answer *"No!"* We cannot blame others because we do not respond well to what they do. Each of us is accountable for our responses.

Justifiable Stealing?

Perhaps you remember the 2005 news report of the housekeeper who worked for celebrities and was caught stealing tens of thousands of dollars in jewelry, clothes, and credit cards. She admitted the thefts, but justified herself, saying, *"I only stole from people who didn't treat me with respect."* After stealing a $96,000 pair of diamond earrings from Robert De Niro's wife, the thief excused her actions to the police, explaining, *"If she treated with more respect, I probably wouldn't have done this."* She insisted that she never robbed people who treated her nicely.[5]

In this case, fortunately, the courts did not accept the thief's excuses. Her thinking does illustrate the thoughts of many lawbreakers—she saw herself as a victim, which gave her the right to steal from the "perpetrators." She is typical of most criminal types, who justify their actions by blaming the victim. You may hear them say things such as, *"He was asking for it… That's what they get for being the way they are… Hey, I've got a hard life and she's got it easy… I only took it because they didn't pay me what I earned… They were too stupid to protect their stuff, so they deserved to lose it."* People with "victim" thinking hate to feel guilty, so they must justify themselves in order to excuse their misdeeds. Whatever their bad choices, it is always someone else's fault.

"You are to blame for my bad language."

In Florida, *Palm Beach Post* reporters were excluded from a year-end interview session with Governor Jeb Bush because the newspaper's bureau chief had cursed at the governor's communications director in a phone call. The disrespectful behavior had lost the *Post* access to the governor. The *Post's* deputy managing editor pined, *"It's just sad that the governor's office would take an action which in effect punishes the readers and the public in Palm Beach County and Martin County."*[6]

Rather than acknowledge that the privileged access was lost because his reporter behaved badly, he accused the governor's office of punishing the readers. The deputy managing editor saw the *Post* reporter not as the perpetrator of irresponsible behavior who reaped a consequence for his readers, but as a victim of the governor. It was, however, his employee who misbehaved—not the governor's office. The offending reporter should have been required to apologize to the readers for "punishing" them.

As long as parents, journalists, liberal judges, and politicians continue to treat perpetrators like victims and excuse them from exercising self-control when offended, we will continue to watch the fabric of our society weaken.

A Nation of Victims

A victim mentality permeates much of our modern family life and society. Many parents foster in their children this mindset by excessive coddling, rewarding excuses, and rescuing them from opportunities for character development. Politicians and social activists carry a similar approach into government, which impacts our schools, our courts, and our social programs. We have become a culture of victims.

Charles J. Sykes, in his book *A Nation of Victims*, points out that in the last fifty years Americans have been losing their sense of personal responsibility.[7] He noted that as mental health experts have emphasized the psychological causes for our behaviors, we have ceased to accept responsibility for our actions and reactions. We have come to see ourselves as "victims" and blame outside influences or genetic predispositions for what we think and what we do. That is why, as Sykes points out, we have become such a litigious society. In 1960, less than 100,000 federal lawsuits were filed; in 2000, there were more than 265,000.[8] Such a litigious society exists only because people are greedy and want to believe that someone else is responsible for them.

Consider the types of lawsuits that have made the news in recent years. People believe fast food restaurants should have to pay for their problem with overeating; gun-makers should be held responsible because someone was irresponsible or lacked self-control; "big tobacco" should compensate the families of those who enslaved themselves to smoking. The news is sprinkled with stories these days about people who believe they should not be held accountable for their vices, actions, or reactions. Over the last few years I have collected dozens of related articles that reveal "victim thinking." Here are summaries of a few. See how quickly you can spot the victim element in each.

In 2006, a New York administrative law judge decided that a worker with the Department of Education deserved only a reprimand, after being fired for disregarding supervisors and continuing to surf the Internet during work hours.[9]

Apparently, laziness and defiance are no longer sufficient grounds for dismissal. And neither is stealing, since the lazy worker took paychecks from his employer, yet failed to provide the hours of service for which he was hired. The judge apparently thought the fired employee was a victim of an unjust employer — his judgment penalized the party who behaved responsibly and rewarded the party who was irresponsible.

An arbitrator ruled that a Michigan parole officer could get his job back, along with back pay and a raise. He had been fired after computer logs showed he had been surfing the Internet four hours a day, visiting X-rated Web sites during work hours. The arbitrator thought firing was too harsh for a first-time offense.[10]

Since the fired worker was a parole officer we should hope he had a functioning sense of right and wrong. If so, then he ostensibly knew he was deceitfully breaking a rule to ogle pornography when he was supposed to be working. Logically speaking, failing to provide a service for which one has been hired and receiving paychecks for hours not actually worked constitutes stealing. For justice to have been served he should have been fired and then required to reimburse his employers for the amount of pay he stole from them.

Tavis Smiley, a black talk show host and liberal political activist, moderated a 2007 Democrat presidential debate, but was unwilling to request the predominantly black audience to honor the no-applause rule. He explained that it was "because black people are an emotional people. I know it wouldn't have worked." He was certain African-Americans would have been unable to control themselves, because of what he called their "emotional" inclinations, and, therefore, didn't ask them to keep a basic rule of order.[11]

Mr. Smiley effectively created an excuse for blacks, regarding them as victims of their emotional nature, and, therefore, exempt from restraining themselves. I doubt he meant to demean his fellow African-Americans by insinuating that as a people they lacked inner controls, but his statement was clear. I don't know if any in the black community publicly objected to the stereotype Smiley put forth, but they certainly should have found his remarks insulting. By creating this exemption, Mr. Smiley exemplified what has happened throughout our culture. When we assume people lack the ability (or willingness) to keep a rule, be it civil or social, we don't hold them accountable—instead we throw out the rule.

In 2005, after Hurricane Katrina, there was widespread looting in New Orleans. News cameras even caught some police officers participating in the thefts.[12] International singing star Celine Dion, however, said she had no problem with people taking things without paying for them. "Oh, they're stealing twenty pair of jeans or they're stealing television sets. Who cares? They're not going to go too far with it. Maybe those people are so poor, some of the people who do that they're so poor they've never touched anything in their lives. Let them touch those things for once."[13]

It seems Ms. Dion forgot that when someone steals, someone else loses. I have to wonder—would she have been so generous if they were stealing everything from her home? Just as good parents teach their children that lack does not excuse stealing, we must reinforce in our society that poverty never justifies theft. Poverty neither creates nor excuses bad character, and neither does a crisis.

In Florida in 2007, a sixty-one-year-old woman was arrested for shoplifting from a grocery store. She tried to justify her actions by explaining that she had Irritable Bowel Syndrome, and was unable to wait in lines.

Fortunately for the town of Cape Coral, neither the police nor store officials felt her condition exempted her from obeying the law.[14]

Obviously, the woman needed to justify to herself why she was shoplifting, and her physical malady seemed like a good excuse. I'm sure Irritable Bowel Syndrome is a very uncomfortable condition, and long checkout lines must be very challenging. However, I would guess that most IBS sufferers out there have found legal ways of obtaining food.

Here are some other examples of "victim thinking" from around the world: In the UK, a teenager planned for days to find a black woman on the streets to murder. He finally found his victim and knifed her to death. His attorney blamed the crime on his client's paranoid delusions and schizophrenia, which created an obsession with the violent video game Grand Theft Auto.[15]

This young man was portrayed not as a perpetrator of murder, but a victim under the influence of a violent game. I'm sure the murder victim's children and grandchildren found no consolation when they heard that there was no perpetrator in the crime—only two victims.

In Penryn, Cornwall, England, nineteen-year-old Tommy Kimpton killed seventeen-year-old Ben Williams in retaliation for many years of taunting and bullying. After a night of drinking and smoking marijuana together, Kimpton bludgeoned Williams to death with a pool cue. Kimpton hid the body and then attempted suicide. The court decided that because Kimpton had been a victim of so much bullying in his life, he was not entirely responsible for his actions and should not be charged with murder. He was found guilty of manslaughter and sentenced to life in prison with a chance for release in two-and a-half years.[16] This is representative of a movement to create a new class of victims to be exempted from personal responsibility — "bully victims."

In Sweden a forty-two-year-old man was diagnosed as disabled because of his addiction to heavy metal music. This qualified him for wage supplements from the Employment Service Job Center. It also forced his employer to allow him to play loud rock music at work and accommodate his attendance at rock concerts. In 2006, he went to almost three hundred shows.[17]

A former councilman in Scotland was accused of frightening his government colleagues by using CAPITAL letters for EMPHASIS in his emails. Although none of his messages contained any kind of threats, officials said they felt intimidated by his use of CAPITAL letters. This resulted in a formal complaint filed with the Standards Commission and an investigation.[18] It sounds to me like a clear case of "YOU are responsible because WE lack the maturity to handle CAPITALS." Poor babies.

A man who discovered his wife was having an affair was forbidden by British courts from making public the name of the man with whom she committed adultery. The judge declared, "There is a powerful argument that the conduct of an intimate or sexual relationship is a matter in respect of which there is 'a reasonable expectation of privacy'."[19] The magistrate apparently judged the male adulterer to be not a perpetrator deserving of discipline, but a victim of bad choices who needed to be protected from suffering the consequences of those choices.

Liberals, because of their misguided commitment to indulgent love, are strong promoters of victim thinking. Because of their blindness, I don't have much hope of convincing them that they are harming the very country they care about, but I do hope that conservatives do not become intimidated, fearing they might appear to be uncompassionate or hateful. It is imperative that conservatives continue to emphasize personal responsibility, both in their homes and in their communities.

Warped View of Compassion

One of the caricatures of liberals is that they are *soft on crime*. If there is any truth to that it is only because of their indulgent view of compassion. To a liberal parent it seems cruel to force children to endure something they don't like; it seems harsh to subject them to firm disciplinary consequences for disobedience; and it feels heartless to permit them to cry over something the parent has the power to change. As I have sought to emphasize, character is developed through handling disappointment and hardships. We deprive our children of developing the character they need when we shelter them from too many of the challenges of life, particularly when we exempt them from the consequences of their behavior. It takes selfless love on a parent's part to not cave in and rescue children from things that make them unhappy.

One of the factors that makes parents soft on discipline is that they are insecure and need their children's approval. Liberals in the political *parent* role are no different—their need for acceptance or popularity compels them to offer weak, indulgent leadership to those in the *child* role. Their insecurity forms their worldview and literally causes them to see *semi* victims as *full* victims. They feel so badly for the "victims" because of the oppression they have suffered or the pain they have brought upon themselves that they give them special treatment and exempt them from responsibility. A parent might say *"I love them so I don't want them to face this hardship."* A liberal in the *political parent* role might say, *"They've had life so hard, it would be unkind to not make their life better."* Such a style of leadership promotes victim thinking, and causes the semi victims to think that they are entitled to special treatment.

There is a direct relationship between soft parenting and mushy justice. The same individuals who are afraid to be firm with their children are always fearful of being too tough on law-breakers. Their sense of justice is skewed by their mushy view of love. Just as they are hesitant to discipline misbehaving children, they feel sorry for convicted criminals and therefore want to limit the consequences they reap for their crimes. After all, they reason, criminals are only bad because they are victims of their backgrounds. How can we justifiably punish people who are not entirely responsible for their behavior?!

Suffering in Paradise

While in Hawaii recently, I saw a severe homeless problem on Oahu that I had not seen in my previous trips. In the Waianae area on the west side of the island, there are beautiful day-use parks at the ocean's edge. For many years their grassy lawns and shade trees had made them popular picnic areas for both locals and tourists. However, recently the homeless and transient population has created unsightly, ragtag tent cities, despite the posted "No Camping" signs. The parks' newly transplanted coconut trees and shrubbery are dying because vagrants continue to shut down the sprinkler system to keep their tents dry. The restrooms, designed for light visitor use, are now in constant disrepair because of 24/7 cooking and showering. Tourists see the hobo village with dying trees, and have the option to keep on driving. Locals, however, are quite frustrated—they can no longer picnic freely in their own neighborhoods, because of the hordes of homeless camped out on the lawns. With so many campers drunk or high, and car break-ins frequent, locals stay away for fear of personal safety. In this tropical paradise, some of the most beautiful beach parks have been taken over by vagrants and crime.

Why, you might wonder, don't the police just arrest violators of the camping laws? I have to assume, from what you have read thus far, that you can guess the answer. Those in authority have decided that these vagrants are "victims" who have a hard life, and it would be cruel to require them to obey the law. Besides, among the vagrants are a few who have actually lost their homes and truly are "unsheltered." In the eyes of the undiscerning they are *all* victims of hard times. I do believe that the truly unsheltered deserve help, but at Waianae parks they are lawbreakers. Does it surprise you to hear that when local citizens complain to authorities about the overrun parks and increased crime, they are rebuked and made to feel guilty for having no heart for the "down and out."

Liberals scold and intimidate anyone who suggests that semi victims should take responsibility for themselves. With talk of caring for the needy, and holding out the genuinely unsheltered as poster children, liberals do seem compassionate. But their approach to leadership actually fosters irresponsibility and ungratefulness. In this case, they are choosing criminals over law-abiding citizens. The result of such "compassion" is that justice and reason are set aside.

Soft on Crime

Mushy justice is part of modern thinking, and is rampant in the courts. Not only do defense attorneys increasingly present their clients as victims, but liberal judges and juries are inclined to render verdicts as if they were indulgent parents. It seems that every day in the news we read about one miscarriage of justice after another.

In 2006, a Vermont court found thirty-four-year-old Mark Hulett guilty of repeatedly raping a little girl over a four-year period, starting when she was seven years old. Despite Hulett's confession, Judge Edward Cashman announced to the courtroom that he no longer believed in punishing such criminals. "The one message I want to get through is that anger doesn't solve anything," he explained to the supporters of Hulett's victim. He therefore sentenced Hulett to sixty days in jail to be followed up with treatment for his sexual disability. Cashman made clear that he no longer believed punishment was an effective deterrent to this type of crime.[20]

In 2007, a man from Severna Park, Maryland, was found guilty of molesting his daughter over a seven-year period, beginning when she was eight. His crime also included molesting two of his nieces. Defense attorney Roger Harris Jr. argued that his client's sexual deviance was comparable to alcohol and drug addiction. Convinced that the molester was a victim of addictive behavior and therefore a candidate for rehabilitation, Judge Joseph P. Manck sentenced him to four months in jail and eight months under house arrest. His sentence included a work-release arrangement that permitted him to leave jail each day to carry on his job as a real estate agent.[21] Even if the pedophile was totally repentant and no longer a threat to children, in any society such atrocities against innocent children deserve severe punishment.

At Columbia University in October 2006, student protestors disrupted an event opposing illegal immigration. Speaker Marvin Stewart's speech was interrupted with heckling shouts, clapping, and other antics. Finally, while Minuteman Project founder Jim Gilchrist was addressing the audience, about twenty protestors rushed the stage in an effort to communicate their own message and shut down the event. It was a violent confrontation that forced security guards into a struggle with the protestors. School officials waited six months before administering discipline to three of the protestors.[22] These students, ostensibly demonstrating no understanding of the First Amendment, had behaved like spoiled children who wouldn't tolerate any opinions other than their own. They brought shame on the university by their disrespect of university guests and their apparently violent, defiant actions merited expulsion, if not arrest. Instead, three of them received simple warnings.

On April 18, 2001, fifty student protestors at Harvard University stormed an administration building and staged a disruptive sit-in for three weeks. They were trying to force their will upon the university regarding an increase in the campus minimum wage. Outside the building, protestors simultaneously set up a tent city and held rallies in support of the cause. President Neil L. Rudenstine said that the protestors have had a right to their opinions, but that "it is not their right to occupy a University building, to interfere with the conduct of work inside it, and to disrupt the lives of nearby student residents, in an effort to force a different decision." The president, nevertheless, allowed the protestors to remain in the building for three weeks, even permitting food and restroom breaks.[23] Strong words, but by allowing the trespassers to remain in the administration building for three weeks, even permitting food and restroom breaks, Rudenstine coddled them and reinforced that it was their right to defy authority.

The only way to teach such students responsibility is to make them face the consequences of their actions. They should have been arrested for trespassing, disorderly conduct and disturbing the peace. If the students had chained themselves to the furniture and there was no way to physically remove them, then they should have been forced to go without food or bathroom breaks until they felt compelled to release themselves. Their discomfort would have been their choice—it is part of sacrificing for a cause. As it was, they were made comfortable and were ultimately rewarded for their defiance.

Harvard is a private institution and is accountable not to the students, but to its governing body. As a private organization they can choose to do business as they please and pay their employees minimum wage if they choose. Just as the university is not coercing people to work there, it is not forcing students to attend. Students who do not like the way Harvard does business can find another college more to their liking. If enough students leave in protest, Harvard, or any business for that matter, will get the message and make whatever changes are necessary to regain business. Until we cease rewarding lawbreakers and start consistently holding them accountable, we will not see moral growth in our society.

In the summer of 2006, Ohio teens Dailyn Campbell and Jesse Howard played a prank that critically injured two people. The boys had labored to create a realistic-looking deer and placed it in the road to watch as cars swerved to avoid it. This caused an accident that left a driver with multiple broken bones, including a broken neck, and his passenger with brain damage. The pranksters pleaded no contest to vehicular vandalism among other charges. Judge Gary McKinley sentenced the boys to sixty days in a juvenile detention center and gave them the assignment of writing a five-hundred-word paper entitled "Why I Should Think Before I Act." However, knowing the boys to be standout football players on the Kenton High School team, and with the season just starting, Judge McKinley decided that they should begin serving their sentences at the conclusion of the football season. He excused his decision saying, "I shouldn't be doing this, but I'm going to."[24] He knew his decision was wrong, but apparently, since their irresponsibility already damaged the lives of two innocent people, he reasoned that the team be shouldn't be penalized nor should the boy's future football prospects be jeopardized. Besides, the judge saw "positive things about participating in football." It was classic victim-thinking—there were already two victims—why make more?

In Escambia County, Florida, Judge William White is determined to deter people from driving drunk by means of public embarrassment, so he orders some drivers to attach a bumper sticker to their car that asks "HOW'S MY DRIVING? THE JUDGE WANTS TO KNOW!!!" It gives an ID number and a phone number.

Needless to say, public guardians of self-esteem are trying to help drunk drivers keep their dignity by fighting the stickers. The same folks are up in arms about Judge Ted Poe of Houston, now a congressman, who has employed a similar strategy. He ordered a drunk driver to hold a sign in front of a bar that read, "I killed two people while drunk driving." He also once had a man make a public apology on the steps of city hall after beating his wife. In 2001, a Corpus Christi judge began having pedophiles post signs in their yards that identified them as registered sex offenders. The threat of public embarrassment successfully intimidates some into thinking twice before they take risks, but those who value the self-esteem of lawbreakers more than the safety of the community will always fight such measures.

Not every judge or jury in the country is soft on crime. However, until our society regains a basic understanding of personal responsibility we should expect to see more and more examples of convoluted justice in our courts.

How We Create a Victim Culture

Cultivating victim-thinking starts when our children are young. If we are insecure and need their affection, we look for reasons to exempt them from responsibility or discipline. To justify ourselves we make excuses for them. When our children misbehave we say things like, *"She's just cranky, because she missed her nap." "He hasn't had his meds today." "She's just high-strung." "Well, boys will be boys." "His teacher just has it out for him." "She just has lots of energy." "He sometimes acts out because his brothers always pick on him."* On occasion those things may be true, but excuses do not exempt us from personal responsibility. People who are cut slack time and again come to see themselves as unaccountable for their choices and decisions. If they *are* held accountable, they are aghast, and feel like victims of injustice.

A friend of mine who teaches English literature at a local junior college recently shared with me how students had changed over the years. A look of amazement came over her face as she told of the dramatic transformation that had occurred. Twenty years ago, she said, students generally accepted lower grades when they scored poorly on tests or failed to complete assignments on time. Rarely did any challenge her—most took a low grade as a sign that they needed to work harder. Now, she says, it is common for students to protest low grades. They know they need higher grades to get into a four-year school, so they charge into her office and insist that she raise their grade. No matter how clearly she explains the concepts of personal responsibility, they seem unable to comprehend that higher grades must be *earned*—low grades cannot be raised on the basis of good excuses for poor test scores and tardy assignments. When she sweetly, but firmly, refuses to give them what they have not merited, they leave her office frustrated, feeling like victims of an unreasonable, cold-hearted professor. Apparently, too many people in the past rewarded their excuses.

Excuses, Excuses

Just as parents make excuses for their children and students make excuse for themselves, our courtrooms have become a showcase of excuse-making. Dr. Tom O'Connor, program manager of Criminal Justice and Homeland Security and director of the Institute for Global Security Studies at Austin Peay State University, in a lecture to his students listed sixty-five "syndromes" and "conditions" people have claimed in courts to exempt themselves from responsibility. Some are legitimate conditions, but the claimants blamed the affliction for their behavior. Here are just a few:[25]

> **Adopted Child Syndrome:** claims a "sleeper effect" in knowledge of being adopted leading to crime.

American Dream Syndrome: claims cultural influence of wanting to get ahead economically causes crime.

Arbitrary Abuse of Power Syndrome: claims behavior due to dealing with bureaucrats all day.

Battered Child Syndrome: used as excuse for stepkids who kill their stepparent(s)

Chronic Lateness Syndrome: used in 1992 to explain a fired Chicago school teacher's tendency to arrive late. Admitted as attempt at justification.

Computer Addiction: a claim that point-and-shoot computer games cause violence.

Distant Father Syndrome: invented by Robert Bly in book *Iron John* (1993) and explains crime as vindictiveness toward an absent father who never paid child support and never showed son his workplace.

Drug Abuse Defense: (*People v. Richard* 1989, CA) often the claim of child molesters that they are not responsible because they were high on drugs at the time, generally unsuccessful.

Failure-to-File Syndrome: a NY University professor, Steve Coleman, used this in 1994 to explain an overall inability to act in one's best interests, all the while being highly anxious about it. It has been successful in a number of cases, but has yet to be applied to criminal tax cases.

Meek-Mate Syndrome: first invoked by a California man in 1994 who killed his wife because she psychologically emasculated him by calling him names, ridiculing him in public, and forcing him to sleep on the floor.

Mother Lion Defense: seeks to justify mother's violent reactions taken to protect her children. Often admitted and successful.

Parental Abuse Syndrome: the Menendez defense, successfully used to claim that years of emotional, physical or sexual abuse by a parent on a child causes loss of control over later behavior.

Premenstrual Stress Syndrome: hormonal changes are so severe that a woman is driven to the unthinkable. Used successfully to acquit Virginia surgeon Geraldine Richter in 1991 for a DUI arrest and Zsa Zsa Gabor-type behavior.

Rock and Roll Defense: alleges that subliminal messages in rock, or in some cases rap, music, were the cause of conduct. Used in Manson defense (Beatles), Judas Priest (1990), and Tupac Shakur music.

Roid Rage: (violence caused by steroids), coined by Dr. David Datz, Harvard Medical School, anabolic steroids typically cause aggression. Used successfully in 1993 in California to explain a bodybuilder's uncontrollable rage in strangling his girlfriend to death.

Self Victimization Syndrome: a sociological phenomenon that explains constant anger and unhappiness with one's place in society, also known as cycle of poverty defense. A few cases won with it in D.C. and CA.

Twinkie Defense: in 1978, Dan White was found guilty of involuntary manslaughter instead of first-degree murder for the killing of San Francisco Mayor George Moscone and Supervisor Harvey Milk. At the time immediately before the killings, Dan White only consumed junk food.

The compulsion to devise excuses to escape consequences has been happening since Adam blamed Eve for his decision to eat the forbidden fruit. However, it seems that in our psychologically-based, victim-oriented culture we have developed excuse-making into an art form.

Curing Victim Thinking

In our society, victims of circumstances can be taught personal responsibility the same way children are taught. We must not do for our children tasks they need to do for themselves. If they break something, they must repair it; if they dirty something, they must clean it; if they lose or steal something, they must replace it; if they leave something on, they must go back and turn it off; if they leave a door open, they must go close it; if they incur a debt, they must pay it.

We must not constantly rescue our children, but allow them to reap what they have sown. If they habitually dawdle and miss their ride, don't automatically drive them; if they continually procrastinate and leave their homework to the last minute, don't do it for them; if they make an unwise business decision, or make a foolish purchase, let them live with their choices; if they are in trouble at school, don't automatically take their side; if their behavior lands them in jail, don't bail them out; if they are sexually promiscuous, do not provide them birth control; if your daughter is pregnant, don't help her abort the child.

Parents, politicians, teachers, judges, and social activists must learn that it is unloving to reward defiance of authority or irresponsibility. When we continually reward irresponsibility by removing natural consequences, it harms the very ones we want to help by encouraging laziness and dependence. Those who are continually rescued from consequences grow in their sense of self-importance and come to believe indulgence is their supreme right. And if the consequences they avoid are *civil* and not *natural*, the effect is even worse on society.[26]

CHAPTER NINE

DEFENSIVE PARENTING

*"If you want to see Mommy Jekyll become Mother Hyde,
just mess with her kids."*[1]

L UANNE, A FRIEND OF MINE, once had an experience at the
zoo that will send chills down the spine of many parents.
It is so incredible that I'm not sure I would believe it if I
hadn't heard it directly from Luanne and her son.

One day in 1994, Luanne and eight-year-old Michael visited the
local zoo. At one point during their outing they found themselves in
a crowd watching a zookeeper move a young tiger between cages.
In spite of the handler's efforts to keep control as he opened the cage
door, the animal managed to break free and escape. Everyone
watched helplessly as the tiger lunged into the crowd and pounced
on the most vulnerable prey it could see—Luanne's son. Without a
second thought, 5' 4" Luanne grabbed the tiger by the scruff of the
neck and by the tail, and walked it backward through the open cage
door where the stunned zookeeper took control. Unharmed and
grateful that the tiger submitted to her control, Luanne went back to
check on her son, who, fortunately, was only dazed by the
experience.

When the crowd finished sucking air, they broke into applause,
having witnessed a phenomenon beyond any they had observed in
the animal kingdom that day. They had seen a diminutive human

mother draw upon a reserve of fearlessness and strength to protect her child from imminent threat. Luanne had only done what would be in the hearts of any parent to do—at risk of her own life, she leaped to the rescue of her innocent child.

Wimps and Tigers

Yes, it is good and natural when parents passionately defend their children. However, indulgent parents go way beyond natural defensiveness. Because they are so committed to their children's happiness, they don't just protect their children from all *physical* threats—they ardently and habitually defend them from all *emotional* distress. If the offender is their child's playmate, they run to the rescue and scold the little troublemaker. If it is the playmate's mother, they have no qualms about giving her a piece of their mind. If their child complains about someone in authority— teachers, coaches, or law enforcement officials—indulgent parents automatically assume their child's innocence and attack the one who suggests otherwise. To these overly defensive parents, their children are never completely responsible for what they have done. There is always an excuse for questionable behavior. "They just need to be understood."

Indulgent parents are a combination of two extremes—they are *wimps*, but they are also *tigers*. They are indulgent and lenient with their children, but dangerous to anyone who threatens their children's happiness. The indulgent attitude that makes them soft also makes them dangerous.

Nancy Gibbs, in an article on indulged children in *Time* magazine, writes about this parenting phenomenon:

> It is a natural, primitive instinct to want to make your child happy and protect him from harm or pain. But that instinct, if not tempered, also comes with a cost. Adolescents can't learn to become emotionally resilient if they don't get any practice with frustration or failure inside their protective cocoons. Sean Stevenson, a fifth-grade teacher in Montgomery County, Md., says parents always say they want discipline and order in the classroom, but if it's their

child who breaks the rules, they want an exemption. "They don't want the punishment to be enforced," says Stevenson. "They want to excuse the behavior. 'It's something in the child's past. Something else set him off. He just needs to be told, and it won't happen again'."[2]

It was this teacher's observation that parents say they value discipline, but when it comes down to it, they want *their* child exempted. Knowing what is right, and having the objectivity to follow through, are two different things. Indulgent parents, because they lack impartiality, have no clue to their child's character deficiencies or to how they are helping create them. The same defensiveness that blinds parents to the faults of their child keeps them from seeing their own mistakes in parenting. Such parents are highly resistant against any inference that there is something wrong with their parenting or their children. All they know is that they love their kids and want good for them—and it seems that's all they *want* to know.

That defensive mindset makes a book like this difficult for many parents to read. The multiple inferences in these pages that their child is lacking or that they have made mistakes in their parenting will turn the wimp into the tiger. Those of you who have read this far without throwing the book against a wall are doing well.

As a pastor I have been speaking into people's lives for many years, and believe me, I have seen this phenomenon too many times. Most people who want help in their personal lives are open to being admonished about areas of weakness. Yet, some of the same people who thank me for confronting them about bitterness, lust, or selfishness, will quickly rise up in anger when I speak to them about their little ones. When the issue is *children* the tiger comes out immediately.

Parental Blindness

As a result of victim thinking, insecurity, or a confused view of family loyalty, indulgent parents are hyper-defensive and lack objectivity. In the eyes of the indulgent parent, the child is always innocent or misunderstood, and those who suggest otherwise are the enemy. Since they view their child as a victim deserving of extra sensitivity, they become apologetic to the child if they feel forced to administer some kind of disciplinary consequence. Needless to say, when someone outside the family subjects their child to disciplinary action, they cry "no fair," and in classic victim thinking, they blame the enforcers of the discipline.

Do you remember the news story in early 2007 about the hyper-defensive parents in Italy? In the town of Bari, parents held a middle school principal responsible for the low grades earned by their child. The father and two other male relatives went to the school and beat up the administrator, sending him to the hospital. They justified the assault, citing the bad report card and their child's unhappiness with the school's recent ban on cell phones.[3] Although disappointed with their child's academic performance, these parents were so deluded by their victim perspective that they held responsible the one reporting grades rather than the one who earned them. It was a classic case of "shooting the messenger."

When I was in high school our basketball team easily beat a rival school one night, but it was only easy because the other team had played without its two best players for most of the game. The two had broken training, and their coach had benched them for the first three quarters. After the game, parents berated the losing coach, because they felt he had punished the entire school—not just the two players. The parents obviously had no grasp that it was not the coach, but the two boys who had been careless and put the team at risk. It was the two boys who had made choices that hurt others. From the beginning of the season the boys had known the team rules and the consequences. The two players had no gripes with the coach—they were remorseful after seeing what their bad choice had done to the team. The team wasn't upset with the coach. The only ones complaining were the parents, whose understanding of personal accountability was lost amidst their hyper-defensiveness.

That scenario occurred over thirty-five years ago, but if it had happened in a junior sports program in the twenty-first century, the parents would have rioted. Parents out of control at children's events have become so common that I stopped collecting the articles a long time ago. Regularly, the news carries stories of parents who attack referees, who fight each other, and who assault their children's coaches—all because they are defensive of their indulged children.[4] Perhaps you have read the accounts of volatile parents who have even attacked their child's opponents in the middle of a game[5] or who've arranged for a hit man to eliminate their child's chief competition.[6] The violence doesn't just occur at sporting events—sometimes it is a school play, a junior beauty pageant, or even a PTA meeting. Most parents fifty years ago could not have imagined adults with such juvenile, out of control behavior.

It is obvious that the violence we are seeing in these parents is the inevitable expression of a generation of indulged children who have grown up and now have their own children. Having grown up indulged, these parents failed to learn self-control from their own parents, and so have become dangerous spectators for their children's activities. By their example they are insuring that their children will grow up to be even more out of control and dangerous when they become parents themselves.

Tiger Liberals in the Parent Role

Like indulgent parents, liberals are both wimps and tigers. With those in the child role they are wimps, protecting their right to pursue their passions, but with those who oppose the "children's" freedom to express themselves, they rise up and attack like tigers.

I remember a TV newscast of a meeting between city officials, liberal activists, and evangelical Christians to discuss a recent protest that involved the local police. The Christians held an event in their church to discuss certain social issues, which were apparently objectionable to the liberal activists. While the church meeting went on, the liberal activists attempted to disrupt it by making noise and attacking the building. The activists became so violent that they caused significant property damage. When wood splintered and glass started to break, police finally intervened. The protest quickly escalated from protected First Amendment activities to riotous criminal conduct.

This follow-up meeting with city officials was shocking to see. Those who committed the crimes were not dealt with as out-of-control hoodlums but as deprived children who had been victimized by a bully. City officials spoke with syrupy sensitivity, assuring the protestors that they understood how hard their life was. The officials kept apologizing to the protestors that they had to endure such intolerance from people like these Christians. While they fell all over themselves to be sweet and sensitive to the rioters, they were equally as *harsh* to the law-abiding Christians. It seemed that every word the officials spoke to them was angry and accusatory. The city leaders defended their "children," who had misbehaved, and attacked the innocent ones who had "provoked" them to violence. They behaved like insecure parents who needed the approval of their insolent children.

Politicians or judges in the parent role often view liberal rioters or lawbreaking protestors with sympathy and understanding. They see them as victims whose anarchical behavior is merely the outcry of a heart that has endured some kind of injustice, discrimination, or intolerance. Liberals have difficulty causing disciplinary pain for those they feel have already suffered so much or who have risked arrest for a "noble" cause.

Guardians of Self-Esteem

Hyper-defensive parenting, both familial and political, is rooted in the belief that children's feelings of self worth must be protected at all cost. Some are so preoccupied with children's happiness that it becomes a crusade.

Self-appointed guardians of human dignity and self-worth are upset about a new—though relatively obscure—trend in parenting. Recently, parents have used public embarrassment to pressure their children into making better life choices. In April 2007, a Knoxville dad who discovered his fourteen-year-old son was using drugs made him stand in front of Cedar Bluff Middle School wearing a sandwich board that said, *"I abused & sold drugs."*[7] In May 2007, a Temecula, California, mother made her daughter wear a sign that read, *"I engaged in bullying behavior. I got suspended from school.... Don't be like me. Stop bullying."*[8] In February 2006, a Portage, Indiana, sophomore was required by his family to stand in front of their townhouse complex and wear a sign that read, *"I got suspended for using foul language. Look at me now! Don't be like me. Ephesians 4:29."*[9] In 2005, a devoted inner-city mom decided the best way to curb her son's stealing was to have him wear a sign that read, *"Hi!! I'm 13 years old. I steal. I want to go to prison to be with Daddy."* Each of the disciplined young people interviewed said that they felt they had received a just consequence.

In Iowa, one mom who found alcohol under the front seat of her nineteen-year-old son's car didn't prescribe sign-holding for her son. She took out a classified ad to sell the car and explain her son's misdeed. Her ad read, *"OLDS 1999 Intrigue. Totally uncool parents who obviously don't love teenage son, selling his car. Only driven for three weeks before snoopy mom, who needs to get a life, found booze under front seat. $3,700/offer. Call meanest mom on the planet."*[10] Fortunately, she was inundated with calls of support.

Blogs and news site comment boards indicate that the actions of these dedicated parents are supported by many, but there was no shortage of critical comments, revealing that multitudes out there have a mushy view of love and justice.

No Losers

Overly protective parents fail to understand that they are like coaches—their job is to take their children through the training and exercises in childhood that will best prepare them for the challenges of adulthood. If parents or other leaders fail to grasp this, or if they have an imbalanced view of love and justice, they will be tempted to rescue children from all bad feelings—including the negative feelings that may come from *failing* or *losing*.

In the early 1970s, one of my college instructors suggested that the eradication of A-F grading systems, as well as the abolishment of scorekeeping in children's sports, would eliminate losing, and keep children from feeling like "losers." He said that children's self-esteem would suffer unless competition of a serious nature was discouraged. His ideas were the natural outgrowth of the indulgent parenting that began flourishing in the 1960s, and spawned changes in schools and children's sports programs all over the country.

Today in youth sports the emphasis seems to be self-esteem. Trophies, for example, are no longer reserved for winners. It has become common to award each player on a team a trophy—just for participating. In many youth athletic programs the rules have been modified so that all participants can feel more successful. Some baseball leagues don't keep score; some allow all players to bat each inning no matter how many outs; some ban infield chatter lest it distract the batter; and some declare the game over if one team leads by too many runs early in the game. One particular Ohio team—the Columbus Stars—was so talented that league officials ejected them from the schedule midway through the season. They were afraid the Stars' lopsided victories would make the losing teams feel bad.[11] Fear for children's feelings has even caused some elementary schools to outlaw traditional recess games. Dodgeball is often on the "don't play" list because it is "exclusionary" and fosters too much competitiveness.

This is tragic—winning and losing are parts of real life, and children can learn to handle these challenges at a young age. Learning to win with honor develops character, but learning to *lose* gracefully cultivates even more. Let us learn from the example of Thomas Edison who failed countless times in his effort to invent the light bulb, yet famously saw his unsuccessful efforts not as failures, but as *"a thousand ways not to build a light bulb."*[12] Our modern approach not only robs children of important opportunities for personal growth, but reinforces to them that they are not *expected* to have emotional resilience. In my opinion, this low expectation is the chief cause of weakened emotional resilience in our society.

Being Positive

Another way our college instructors encouraged us to strengthen children's self-esteem was to change our terminology. They admonished us to avoid negative words such as "wrong" and "bad" when dealing with children about their behavior. Instead, we were to use only terms such as "unacceptable," "inappropriate," or "not the best." The counselor training I received at the YMCA where I volunteered reinforced what we learned in college. There we were charged with protecting children's feelings about themselves. We were told to never allow them to feel "put down" for any reason—we were to do whatever we could to keep them from feeling judged because of their traits, quirks, or values. This meant we were to discourage all children from stating their own opinions too strongly, lest another child feel unaccepted or put down because he was different. It was inferred that the most uncaring thing we could do for a child was allow to him suffer as a victim of low self-esteem.

Don't get me wrong—I feel awful for children who are always the last one chosen or left out of games. I hate to see children discouraged because they fail in something in which they want to succeed. I have six children—I remember times when I have seen them in tears because they felt like a "loser" or didn't achieve their goals. I have held them in my arms while they cried. Yet I know that to be prepared for real life they must learn to suffer through rejection and to face failures without wallowing in self-pity. They also must discover those things in which they *can* succeed and learn to work hard toward them.

Preserving children from situations that might weaken their self-image and softening the rules to make them feel more like winners has succeeded in boosting our nation's self-worth. *Time* magazine published the results of a study on the correlation of academic success and self-esteem.[13] Charles Krauthammer, the article's author, reported that researchers administered basic math tests to thirteen-year-old students in Britain, Canada, Ireland, Korea, Spain, and the United States. Students were also requested to rate their math skills. American students demonstrated the highest self-esteem, with 68 percent rating themselves as "good at math." However, Americans had the *least* reason to feel good about their math skills—they scored the *lowest*. Other studies reveal the same thing—American students generally have high self-esteem, but lack the performance to substantiate it.[14]

Artificially boosting children's self-image has worked, but to what end! Has it produced a better society? Today's students are academically inferior to those a generation ago. There are nineteen million new cases of STD infections each year.[15] Marriages are weaker—not stronger. The crime rate is significantly higher—not lower. The moral fiber of our nation is slowly deteriorating, and it is due primarily to people thinking too highly and too much of themselves.

Is it Mister Rogers' Fault?

CBS News ran a story on the negative effects the new "positive" approach to child rearing has had in the workplace. Children born between 1980 and 1995, called "millennials," now saturate the job market. According to the report, these workers were *"raised by doting parents who told them they are special, played in little leagues with no winners or losers, or all winners,"*[16] and so present quite a challenge to employers. They are typically demanding, impertinent, and narcissistic. They need constant affirmation and expect to be catered to. Corporations actually hire consultants to teach them how to handle the glut of employees who act like spoiled brats. They can't fire them, because their replacements will have the same entitled outlook on life.

Wall Street Journal columnist Jeffrey Zaslow says, "We can blame Mr. Rogers."[17] I can't say that I agree completely with his assertion, but I have to concur that Mister Rogers typified our modern approach to giving children good feelings about themselves whether earned or not. It wasn't him alone, but he was our mascot. He taught us that special feelings about oneself no longer depended upon character, attitude, or accomplishment—we could feel special for just having a pulse.

With indulgent parenting so prevalent, it is inevitable that children grow up with an exaggerated sense of self-importance. It is no surprise that our jails are full of people with the highest self-esteem.[18] As long as we continue to over-elevate the protection of people's feelings of self-worth, society will reap the bad fruit.

Emotional Resilience

When I was very young, and first discovered the pain of having playmates call me names, my parents passed on to me the sage advice they had received from their parents, which had been passed on from previous generations. They looked me in the eye and said, *"Reb, never forget this: 'Sticks and stones can break my bones, but words will never hurt me.'"* I quickly put it to memory and found myself chanting it to all verbal attackers from that day on. It was a great retort for a four-year-old—I felt well-armed and powerful. But to tell you the truth, my playmates' words and taunts still managed to sting. What I did find, however, was that I didn't have to allow the words to *cripple* me or *shape my identity*. I also found I could survive verbal assaults without calling on my parents to come to the rescue.

I am convinced that I and many more from my generation were able to develop emotional resilience, because we were empowered when our parents treated us like we had the capacity to handle hurt feelings and distress.

I have never considered the insights of a *Star Wars* Jedi knight any more significant than the wisdom in a fortune cookie, but in *The Phantom Menace,* a Jedi offered exceptionally wise words to young Anakin Skywalker. When Anakin was falsely accused by a playmate of cheating, he took offense and sought to defend himself with his fists. Jedi Qui-Gon Jinn responded to Anakin's intolerance of the false accusation, and said, "You *know the truth...You will* have *to tolerate his opinion. Fighting won't change it."* Effectively, he was saying, "You need to learn to live with others' wrong opinions of you." This encapsulates a mature and healthy response to insults, taunts, and lies. We must learn to tolerate others' wrong opinions of us, and teach our children to do the same.

In this current generation I see too many people, young and old alike, who lack emotional resilience. Their parents rescue them whenever another child offends, and they defend them from anyone in authority who tries to hold them accountable for their behavior. These parents, along with teachers and community leaders, were committed to keeping these children happy. It is child-centered leadership that has produced a generation of emotionally weak individuals. It should be of no surprise that indulgent, hyper-defensive parenting is at the root of politically correct speech.

The Basis for Political Correctness

To be politically correct in our speech is to be sensitive to people's feelings. This means we avoid specific words and phrases that particular groups or individuals have decided insult or offend them. These "protected" groups might include races, religions, sexual preferences, or people with unique physical features—anyone, actually, that liberals determine needs protection.

Liberals, you see, own political correctness. They define it and they enforce it—they are in charge of deciding who is to receive PC protection. They are not in charge of it because they thought of it first and beat conservatives to the punch. It is theirs because PC thinking is an inevitable expression of their hyper-defensive view of parenting. Just as liberals view children's feelings as vulnerable, they also relate with adults in the child role as weak and in need of protection, as well. They are people who have never learned to live with others' wrong opinions of them.

This brings us to the very core of PC thinking.

If you have never thought of this before, then consider that political correctness is based on the premise that people—*certain* people—need to be protected from harm. To identify who those *certain* people are, we need only determine who or what in nature needs protection. The answer is obvious—it is the *weak* that need protection. The *strong* certainly do not need it. Propriety teaches us that the strong, in fact, are expected to be sensitive to the vulnerabilities of the weak and protect them.

There you have it.

At the root of political correctness is the assumption that some people are emotionally and socially weak, and, therefore, uniquely vulnerable to getting their feelings hurt. Liberals expect the strong to be sensitive to the emotional vulnerabilities of the weak, lest they suffer hurt feelings beyond their ability to bear.

It is a wonder to me that no one in a protected group has complained of being insulted by politically correct protection. Who in the protected groups would want to be thought of as *weak* or *vulnerable*? How insulting! That, however, is exactly what political correctness is based upon. It says certain people lack the emotional resilience to handle another person's words or opinions. Sticks and stones may break their bones, but apparently words will *kill* them.

Responding to Political Correctness

Believers in political correctness strive to shield the weak from hurt feelings by placing legal restrictions on the strong. But is that wise?

When someone or something is weak and vulnerable, what is really most helpful for them? Is it only to *protect* them or is it to *strengthen* them?

If the vulnerable one is a malnourished child with a weak immune system, do we simply put him in a bubble and keep him away from germs for his entire life, or do we feed him the best nutrition to make him strong? Do we not *strengthen* him rather than merely *protect* him?

Don't we learn from nature that it is best to strengthen the weak rather than shield them forever? An athlete grows stronger and better prepared for challenges by constantly facing them. Our bodies only develop antibodies to disease by encountering germs. Calluses only form to protect our soft tissue because of constant abrasion. Are we not harming the "vulnerable" in our society—weakening their immune systems, you might say—by merely sheltering them from that which has the potential to make them grow? Isn't it obvious that the protectiveness of political correctness makes the weak weaker and preoccupies a culture with its wounds?

When people become *wound*-oriented they grow a huge chip on their shoulder and become hypersensitive to any perceived offenses. Whether they realize it or not, their thin skin is an admission that they lack control over themselves, and the strong have power to determine their well-being. The existence of their "wounds" is a clear acknowledgement that they are weak and helpless, and under the power of the strong. The very idea that the strong are responsible for the responses of the weak is classic victim thinking.

As a result of politically correct thinking in our society, the strong often grow to resent the easily victimized, because they feel forced to "walk on eggshells" lest they accidentally offend. Social unity, consequently, tends to break down, because communities are comprised of those easily offended and those trying not to offend. Today, we are experiencing a subtle social tension that didn't exist fifty years ago.

Where Are We Going?

If we want to know where the U.S. is headed, we need only look across the Atlantic. The U.K. is only steps ahead of us in political correctness. The British government's fear for people's feelings has spawned multitudes of laws and workplace regulations, replete with penalties and fines. They seem obsessed with shielding people in protected groups from offensive words, actions, or beliefs:

> •In December 2007, a student choir was required to change the lyrics of traditional Christmas songs, because administrators feared offending some Christmas concert attendees. Although Christmas is a holiday centered on the birth of the Christ, the choir had to alter any lyrics that actually mentioned the Nativity. For example they had to change "Little donkey, carry **Mary** safely on her way" to "Little donkey, carry **Lucy** safely on her way."[19]

> •In 2006, the Employment Law Advisory Services of Manchester warned against sending Valentine cards to colleagues—they could be interpreted as sexual harassment.[20]

> •In the interest of protecting selected people's feelings, the Lothian and Borders Police Guide instructs police officers not to call elderly people "old," not to refer to women in familiar terms such as "love" or "dear," and not to speak of homosexuals as "homosexual."[21] And neither are they to ask people if they are married, lest they offend homosexuals. Likewise the Department of Children, Schools and Families has released a guidance plan for schools prohibiting use of the terms "Mum" and "Dad" out of sensitivity to homosexuals.[22]

> •A school in Carmarthen, West Wales, has banned the making of Mother's Day cards out of fear that motherless children could be upset by the activity.[23]

> •One September, during the Muslim observance of Ramadan, the National Health Service boards in Greater Glasgow and

Lothian, Scotland, banned staff from eating at their desks, in case any Muslims would take offense during fasting.[24]

•In the U.S., school crowds have been discouraged from booing opposing sports teams,[25] but in Scotland, one school banned children from cheering their own side. Officials feared it might humiliate the other teams. Even more astonishing, at one school in Sutton Coldfield, England, parents were barred from attending a sports day, lest their children suffer embarrassment from losing.[26]

•In Sheffield, England, the District Football League was so concerned about the self-esteem of young players they insisted that the final scores of soccer games not be reported in the press. This was to save the losers embarrassment in case the point spread was extreme. The decision followed a game in which the local paper published the score (29-0) of a game it described as "A Comprehensive Trouncing."[27]

•The home of a woman in Rugby, England, was burglarized, and so she planned to install barbed wire atop her fence. She never did install it, however, because she was warned by law enforcement that she would be subjected to a police investigation should a trespasser injure himself while scaling her fence.[28]

•Police in Coleford, Somerset, witnessed the theft of a moped, but refused to give chase, because the thief was not wearing a helmet. They excused their inaction, saying a chase was too dangerous for the helmetless thief. Police officials defended the officers' inaction, citing the threat of a lawsuit were the thief to get injured in an accident.[29]

•Prisoners in British jails successfully sued the government for forcing them to endure "cold turkey" withdrawal from their drug addictions upon entering jail for miscellaneous crimes. They argued that since they never gave consent to the forced withdrawals, the insensitive treatment they received amounted to assault.[30] The court agreed, and between two separate cases, a total of 198 prisoners were each paid $8,000.

•In Wales, a gang of teenage thugs was terrorizing a quiet neighborhood, causing damage to cars and property, and intimidating the residents. In the U.K., political correctness has placed teenage "children" in a protected class, so complaints to police were to no avail. On one occasion a sixty-four-year-old woman was walking home when a gang of twenty teens blocked her path and taunted her. The harassment became violent, and the grandmother ended up on the ground with a broken arm. She was then arrested on "suspicion of assaulting a minor." On another occasion, a sixty-six-year-old woman spent a night in jail after being pushed by thugs and threatened with a board. Her crime was smacking back at one of the teenage attackers.[31]

There are many who keep shouting, "The emperor has no clothes!" I wonder—will the emperor and his cohorts one day have the courage to look at themselves and see the truth?

Hate Speech

I am certain that by this time, some are misunderstanding my concerns. They think that I am promoting the use of derogatory names and the denigration of people who deserve respect. They might even think I don't care about people's feelings and accuse me of promulgating "hate speech."

Nothing could be further from the truth. Hateful speech is a result of bitterness and arrogance. I loathe the idea of bitter hearts or hateful speech. In fact, I have devoted my life to helping people find Divine love that will heal bitterness and curtail hurtful words.

In my home, we teach our children to speak with consideration at all times—even when angry. This means we forbid them from making fun of anyone and we do not permit them to call people degrading names—even names like *dummy* or *idiot*. We also emphasize overlooking insults—intended or accidental. Kindness is the rule.

If kindness is the standard for my family, you can rest assured that that is how I wish the people of this nation would conduct themselves in their relationships. Kind speaking and merciful responses would eliminate a great many conflicts and heartache.

My chief concern with political correctness, based on all that I have stated in this chapter, is that I don't believe it is wise for the government to try to regulate *politeness*. Parents should teach good manners and society can reinforce them. But once a government makes it illegal to hurt someone's feelings, it is delving into the completely subjective realm of the human heart, and there is no end to what can be outlawed.

Let the government hold us responsible for our immoral actions, for our words that cause physical harm,[32] or for vulgar images and expressions that defile the innocent. But there is no way it can realistically hold us accountable for how others respond to our words, beliefs, or opinions.

To create an arbitrary list of weak members and punish anyone who hurts their feelings is bad parenting and bad government.

CHAPTER TEN

REWARDING BAD BEHAVIOR

"Crime does not pay."[1]

THE UNITED STATES OF AMERICA is a sovereign nation founded on principles of self-determination and personal liberty.[2] Our benevolent government and support of free enterprise provides tremendous opportunities for the success and prosperity of our members, which makes our society an attractive place to live. When our nation was young, our borders were open wide, and all who were able to travel here could make this land their home. As our nation matured, we discovered the need to establish formal citizenship, and we became more discriminating in how we welcomed visitors and processed new members. More recently, with the threat of terrorism, and an influx of immigrants entering the country illegally, we have learned the importance of controlling our borders more carefully. Nonetheless, our borders are crossed without permission by hundreds of thousands each year. Most are from our neighbor to the south—Mexico.

Some Americans say compassion dictates that illegal immigrants be welcomed into the U.S. to receive the blessings that come with the American way of life. They insist upon open borders and total amnesty for those already living here. Their supporters have hosted rallies and sponsored huge marches demanding driver's licenses and jobs, not to mention the right to tax-funded healthcare and education. Former Mexican president Vicente Fox harshly criticized any efforts to stop his citizens from sneaking over the border. He compared the border fence to the Berlin Wall and called it "disgraceful and shameful." Even the European Union foreign policy chief, Javier Solana, has defended illegal immigrants, insisting that they be treated *"like people, not like criminals."*[3]

It is evident from watching the news that illegal immigrants are passionate about their demands for rights.

Many U.S. citizens stand in opposition to such ideas, and don't want to honor demands from those who break the law to cross our border. They insist that since they are "lawbreakers" they should be treated as criminals, and be penalized for their crime. Some have even taken up arms to help patrol the border.[4] Yes, there is great passion on both sides of the illegal immigration issue.

Part of the passion stems from the fact that 68 percent of Mexicans who come to our land enter without permission. According to research of the National Population Council, an agency of the Mexican government, of the eleven million Mexicans living in the U.S., the majority—6.2 million—are here illegally.[5] That number would be greater, but in an average year approximately a million are arrested trying to sneak across the border. In 2005 there were 1.2 million arrested. The bottom line is that the majority of the Mexicans we see around us—almost seven of ten—are here in violation of the law.

Since one of the purposes of this book is to evaluate political perspectives from a parenting standpoint, let's examine the issue of illegal immigration using the framework of proper parenting.

The Rules of our Home

This land—the United States of America—is our home. We as the homeowner have the right to make rules about how everyone is to enter our home. We insist that our neighbors not sneak or barge in, but knock on the front door. If they enter without our permission, we will view them as trespassers. If they take what is not theirs, we will regard them as thieves. If they move into our guest room, we will evict them as squatters. We don't ask much—just that neighbors knock and secure permission before entering our home.

As heads of our home, it is important that our children see we mean what we say. If rules are broken and we fail to bring consequences, the children learn that wrongdoing can be rewarded—that is, we teach them that crime does indeed pay. If it is the neighbors who have broken the rules by sneaking in a window, and we fail to hold them accountable, the neighbors will learn to disrespect us and our authority. In fact, if we tolerate their trespassing, and fail to evict them from the guest room, they will eventually come to think they have a right to be there. In time they will complain about the food and insist that we grant them the same rights as our children. The children will witness our lack of disciplinary action, and have one of two reactions. They will disrespect us for being wimpy in our leadership, or if the neighbors help them with their chores, they may despise us for wanting them gone. One thing is certain—in such a home social chaos will increase as disrespect for authority grows in the children and the uninvited guests.

The principle to remember is this: Those in authority who make rules, but are unwilling to enforce them, *will always lose the respect of those they lead.* Without respect for laws or those responsible to enforce them, families or societies grow out of control.

A Parenting Evaluation of Illegal Immigrants and their Demands

Given the fact that it is illegal to enter our country without our permission, those who do so are lawbreakers. And given the criminal nature of their very presence in the U.S., illegal immigrants have no position to demand anything. In fact, I have to ask—why would we even think of granting citizenship to people who already have demonstrated a severe disrespect for our laws when they violated them to enter our country in the first place?

Do we reward bank robbers by allowing them to keep what they steal? If we advertise a room for rent, will we lease it to the prowler who continually breaks into our home and sleeps on our sofa? Will we not search for a tenant with more character than a proven trespasser?

An illegal alien is someone who has defied American border laws and deceitfully entered this country. That type of entry is no different than someone who climbs in a window of a home with a room-for-rent and begins living there without permission of the owner. Just as there are legal ways of gaining permission to enter a home and rent a room, there are legal ways of entering this country. And just as those who sneak into a home are trespassers and squatters, so also are those who sneak into this country.

There is no flaw in this analogy. It is an exact parallel. It is not that complicated. To be precise, the best term for those who cross our borders without permission is *"border trespasser."* Technically, those who are caught trespassing our borders the first time are committing the federal crime of *entry without inspection*—a misdemeanor. If trespassers are caught violating our borders a second time they are guilty of a felony, and may spend up to two years in jail before they are deported.

Trespassing, whether a felony or misdemeanor, is still a crime that merits civil penalties. If penalties are not dispensed, the results are regrettable.

Trespassers lack humility and have no basis for demands.

When a child is so full of himself that he chooses his own wishes over the rules of his parents, he needs to suffer some kind of disciplinary consequence to restore his humility. Without humility no lessons are learned. The same is true for society's lawbreakers. Those who are convicted of crimes, yet serve their sentence without humility—learn no lessons, and so return to their crimes and to jail, time after time.

One of the concerns I have when I hear border trespassers and their spokesmen on the news is that they lack humility. They are indignant and demanding, as if they have rights to that which is not theirs. At the very least they should be asking for *mercy*—not demanding non-existent "rights." They are *criminals*. No matter how simply they lived in their own country, we owe them nothing except judicial consequences for their crime of illegal entry. They have done wrong. Where is the humility that should characterize a wrongdoer who knows he has done wrong and needs mercy?

Obviously, the humility is absent, because the neighbor has been living in the guest room so long that he thinks he has the right to be here. Either that or he thinks he deserves to be here because we are the "haves" and he is one of the "have-nots." Both perspectives result from indulgent political parenting.

Trespassers sneak into our country and then expect us to give their children food, education, and medical care.

If someone commits a crime and breaks into my home, I am not responsible to feed or care for the children they bring with them while they commit the crime. The criminals are responsible for putting their children at risk—not *me*, the homeowner. Border trespassers put their families at risk by sneaking them into a country where they are not legally permitted to work. It is a foolish man who takes his children into a place where he cannot legally provide for them. It is a cruel man who brings his family with him when he commits a crime—he puts them at risk, and by example teaches them to disregard the law.

Sadly, the U.S. is like a bad parent who coddles his children. If we say, *"Pick up your dirty socks and put them in the hamper or they won't get washed,"* yet we continually pick them up and wash them, we are foolish parents. Children learn to disregard those in authority when they are not required to live with the consequences of their actions. In such homes children never learn personal responsibility, and parents inevitably fail to gain their children's respect.

In the U.S. we forbid deceitful entry, but then we reward the trespassers. We see that they put their children at risk, but instead of sending them packing with a good scolding for endangering their children, we reward them by educating, feeding, and caring for their children. By no means are we obligated to care for children put at risk by their parents, especially if it encourages further irresponsibility in the parents. How blind can we be?

Trespassers expect to receive driver's licenses.

Allowing illegal aliens to acquire driver's licenses is another way we coddle trespassers. It's not that complicated—they are breaking the law. They need to be kicked out of the country—not taught to drive in ours. Yes, registering drivers is a way to ensure safer roads for all who drive them, but they would not be driving our roads if we sent them back to drive in their own country. The principle is sound: *Rewarding wrongdoing promotes more of the same.*

Trespassers are demanding citizenship.

The fact that trespassers are now demanding U.S. citizenship is a direct fruit of our "bad parenting" approach to government. We have coddled and shielded from consequences those who violate our laws, which has caused them to develop a "victim" mentality. Trespassers now see themselves as victims of oppression who deserve special treatment.

What have you learned about creating victims? Enough coddling of irresponsible people and they will come to think they have a "right" to that which they are not willing to acquire properly. We have given trespassers enough special treatment that they now believe they are indeed special and exempted from personal responsibility.

Trespassers blame the U.S., because trespassing is too dangerous.

Jumping the U.S. border is not easy for most. Sometimes trespassers attempt to walk across the desert of southern Arizona and die of exposure—deaths average more than one a day. So many die, in fact, that the Mexican government sponsors community seminars on how to survive the desert route. They also teach trespassers about nutrition, medical care, and managing the stress they will have from living the secret life of an illegal immigrant. They even supply desert-crossers with survival kits, which contain not only food and water, but first-aid supplies and birth control. The kits also include a special card for TB sufferers who plan to get treatment in the U.S., and a list of California health clinics that do not require Social Security numbers.[6] With so much support from their own government, it is no surprise that they feel like victims of U.S. oppression. And neither is it a surprise that when eleven trespassers died of exposure in the desert,[7] sympathizers filed wrongful death lawsuits against the U.S. government for not providing water stations.[8]

Trespassing is a dangerous choice to make. Some illegal immigrants have packed themselves into enclosed trucks like sardines, and have died of heat exhaustion or lack of oxygen. Some travel in more comfortable vehicles, but die in accidents while attempting to escape border patrol agents. In August 2006, an SUV loaded with twenty trespassers crashed when the smuggler tried to outrun the border patrol. Eleven passengers died. Surviving family members refused to hold the smuggler responsible and filed a lawsuit against the agents for trying to stop the fleeing vehicle.[9] A victim mentality is a key element of illegal immigration thinking.

By its very nature crime is dangerous, and when criminals die while committing crimes, it is a victim mentality that says they are not responsible for their own death. The commission of a crime typically requires deception and risk, and invites entanglement with armed law enforcement officials. On multiple levels border trespassers put their lives at risk, but when their gamble doesn't pay off and death results, sympathizers typically do not hold the criminals responsible—they blame the U.S. for making border-crossing difficult.

In my opinion, any death is tragic—even those of criminals in the commission of their crimes. The tragedy is compounded, however, when those who die as a result of risky, illegal choices are held up as the victim, and the U.S. government is portrayed as the perpetrator.

The Mexican government threatens to sue the U.S. over how we handle border trespassers.

On May 15, 2006, President George W. Bush gave a speech on immigration in which he announced the deployment of National

Guard troops to the Mexican border. With border trespassers facing the threat of deadly force, Mexico's Foreign Minister Luis Ernesto Derbez promised, *"If there is a real wave of rights abuses, if we see the National Guard starting to directly participate in detaining people...we would immediately start filing lawsuits through our consulates."*[10] That statement is amazing to me. The government of Mexico believes that their citizens have a *right* to trespass and threatens a lawsuit if we use force to guard our borders. Obviously, the Mexican government has an indulgent style of leadership and views their people as victims.

Let's place this scenario in your neighborhood.

If you find out that your neighbor's children have been sneaking into your yard and camping in your fruit orchard, wouldn't it be natural to appeal to him to get control of his children? If you discover that the children have not only been camping, but picking your fruit and taking it home to sell at their father's fruit stand, wouldn't it be within your rights to build a fence and buy a guard dog?

What would you say if, after building the fence, your neighbor threatens you with a lawsuit for putting barbed wire on the fence, since his children might get injured climbing over it? Wouldn't you consider it his responsibility to provide for his children and keep them out of your yard? If he cannot control his children, would it be unreasonable to expect him to build a fence himself?

Yet, here is the government of Mexico with a victim mentality! Rather than apologize for not securing their own border and keeping better control of their citizens, the Mexican government strangely believes that it is the duty of the U.S. to care for their people. They are even threatening lawsuits if we try too hard to protect our borders.

Rather than making threats against us, Mexican officials should warn their own people about the consequences they will face if they trespass into their northern neighbor's yard. Apparently, they are coddling parents and neglect their own duty, because they desire for their citizens a life not to be found under their own leadership. They then demand that their U.S. neighbor provide that which they are failing to provide themselves. But obviously, we won't see them warn their people—they crave the millions of dollars sent back home into Mexico each year.

As long as America tolerates the commission of border crimes, and rewards the criminals by caring for them and their children, we should not expect to see our nation grow in moral fiber. Such leadership is bad parenting and bad government. May we wake up and do the right thing before it is too late!

CONCLUSION

WE HAVE LEARNED that every generation of adults reflects the parenting approach of those who raised them. People grow up to conduct themselves as citizens and politicians according to the worldview they developed from their upbringing. Societies, therefore, will generally thrive if parents pass on self-control and selfless concern for others, but will suffer moral decline if parents raise children with an over-exalted sense of their own importance. Ultimately, the power to shape a nation is in the hands of parents.

For parents to cultivate good character, they must understand that from birth children are hedonistic and self-centered—by nature they want pleasure without consequence. If parents indulge their children's bent for gratification, and don't make them "suffer" through daily chores and eating their vegetables, the children grow up believing that it is their right to have what they want and that they shouldn't have to suffer consequences for their actions. Although they reach adulthood, their worldview remains that of an untrained toddler—they lack the key ingredients of maturity: self-control, wisdom, and responsibility.

Such adults will either continue in the "child" role and demand gratification without consequence or they will assume the "parent" role and live to indulge those in the "child" role. In this worldview passion trumps reason and logic.

When passion and pursuit of gratification rules a citizenry, and those that govern confuse enabling with compassion, all that destroys a society thrives: crime escalates, addictions soar, mental health breaks down, marriages fail, education suffers, and social chaos ultimately ensues. The Founding Fathers gave us clear warning.

In a society of those lacking virtue, moral standards become arbitrary and ever-changing. Those who encourage and protect the new morality are seen as heroes and those who call for restraint are the villains. The indulgent protectors see themselves as those who care, but their twisted view of compassion is causing more harm than good.

America is obviously in great trouble. We have wasted millions of dollars and countless years trying to fix our moral problems through education, legislation, and self-esteem affirmation. Yet like Dorothy with her red sequined slippers, parents have had the power to make the changes all along. We must grasp this—*parents have the power to shape our nation!*

Parents don't have complete power

Some, I'm certain, misunderstand my intentions and assume I am suggesting that parents have complete and total control over how their children will turn out. Nothing could be further from the truth.

Children are not dogs to be trained or chemicals to be mixed in a lab. They are people—self-determining individuals who ultimately decide what they will do with the training their parents have sought to give them. Obviously, children are greatly impacted by the training they receive, so we must make the most of the few years we have with them at home. Conservatives can greatly increase the likelihood that their children will grow up conservative, but because of the passion-oriented, liberal leanings of human nature, and our current culture that encourages unrestrained pursuit of passions, parents do not have 100 percent control over how their children finally turn out.

That is why you might occasionally see children from the same family, reared by the same parents, turn out complete political opposites of each other. Conservative parents may seek to give their children mastery over their passions, but passions may ultimately seduce one or all of the children and draw them into a liberal view of life. Occasionally liberal parents may see one of their children grow up and embrace conservative ideals, but in my experience that is not as common. Because a liberal outlook is rooted in the passionate, hedonistic bent of human nature it is more natural for a conservative to slip into liberalism than it is for a liberal to step up into conservatism. When a liberal does change his identification to conservative, it is often because he concludes his core values actually *are* conservative. Either that or he goes through a dramatic "spiritual conversion" that changes his nature and shifts his worldview to one based on personal responsibility and concern for others.

Defensive parents

As I have been emphasizing, improved child rearing would dramatically reduce crime, improve education, strengthen mental health, decrease the spread of STDs, and minimize out-of-wedlock pregnancies. Yet for some it is much easier to put the primary blame on racism, poverty, underfunded education, violent entertainment, or the availability of guns. For those who tend to disavow personal responsibility it is more natural to look elsewhere than it is to accept what is so obvious to the objective eye.

Yes—to be certain—the message of a book like this will be enormously popular with some, but will be absolutely despised by others. Except for those who are ready to do whatever it takes to shape their children's character and the few who are desperate to survive their children, many parents these days don't want to be told they need to change. And they definitely don't want to hear that they are responsible for the moral struggles of the country. Yet, if we are to see any real turnaround, the next generation of parents must change how they rear children. The only government program that might work would be one that trained parents in the principles I elucidated in Chapter Four. Without such training, this generation of parents will be unable to give what they do not have.

I plead with America—this is no time for parental defensiveness! There is too much at stake.

Conclusion

I believe that what I have shared here has the power to change lives, families, and nations. It is my prayer that those who crave such a change will call upon God for the grace to make it happen.

APPENDICES

Appendix A: The story of Junior

Junior is two years old and does not like vegetables, scrambled eggs, or meat loaf. His parents want him to grow up happy, so do not require that he eat anything he does not like. In fact, Mom develops the habit of making dinner in two batches—one for Mom and Dad and one prepared a special way for Junior. Eventually, by the time Junior is four, she finds it easier to prepare meals in just one batch, so the family menu becomes limited to whatever makes Junior happy. Cheeseburgers, pizza, and spaghetti become household staples. When eating out they visit only restaurants approved by Junior. In the interest of health, Mom relies upon candy-flavored vitamins as a nutritional supplement.

Mom and Dad grew up in homes where finances were tight, and both are glad that they make good money, so are able to provide for Junior whatever will make him happy. By the time Junior is seven he has accumulated an enormous collection of toys, a huge video library, and a video game player with every game available. In his room he has a computer and a wide screen plasma television with three hundred satellite channels. If he is not happy with what he has been given he is sure to let his parents know. Whining and complaining are commonly heard at meal times or on birthdays, or any time that things are not to his satisfaction.

Neither of Junior's parents was permitted to speak their minds in their own homes growing up, so they are pleased that their son feels free to articulate his feelings. They were required by their own parents to speak respectfully to adults, and have come to believe that raising Junior the same way would cause him to repress his emotions and possibly warp his psyche. They notice that their home is not always peaceful because of Junior's tendency to speak his mind. At first they worry that they are permitting "sass," but after visiting his school classroom, and seeing that many of the children are similarly outspoken towards the teacher, they accept that that is just how kids grow up these days. They come to believe that such freedom to speak one's mind to those in authority is actually a sign of confidence and healthy communication.

Despite all their efforts to make Junior happy, his parents observe that he is rarely pleased. They decide that Junior is just a high-spirited boy with lots of his own ideas. Because he has a mind of his own, his parents have found that he must be instructed multiple times before he does what he's told. When he is resistant they do not usually get angry at him. Instead, they try to be understanding, ascribing his actions to his moods, developmental stages, or personality quirks. They are completely unaware how much they make excuses for his wrong behavior and bad attitudes.

Since Junior is such an outspoken communicator, his mother understands clearly what makes him happy and what makes him mad. And since she is committed to giving him a happy childhood, she gladly helps him by keeping his room clean and his bed made. Both his parents feel that childhood is a time of life to be carefree and unsaddled with heavy responsibility. They believe that schoolwork offers enough stress, so they do everything they can to rescue Junior from responsibility around the house. This rescuing from stress also means that they replace anything he breaks or loses. Eventually, they will even pay his parking tickets and traffic fines.

Shortly into Junior's first year of junior high school his parents notice that he seems to be becoming more sullen. He no longer views privileges as something to be *earned*, but as *rights* to be demanded. He seems to have developed a sense of entitlement, which means he is generally unappreciative and thankless much of the time. In fact, he demonstrates a particular disdain for his parents. He has been exposed to pornography on the Internet since he was ten, and by fourteen he is dabbling in sex and drugs. The more he dabbles the unhappier at home he becomes.

When he is fifteen he is caught by the police with marijuana, but the judge lets him go with barely a slap on the wrist. The judge explains that it is his professional opinion an adolescent lacks a fully developed frontal brain lobe and is not yet capable of understanding the consequences of his impulsive actions. Junior is thrilled that the arrest does not even go on his record.

When Junior turns sixteen he receives a car for his birthday—it is just what he wanted. Sadly, within the first month he has an accident and totals his brand new car. Rather than have Junior get a part-time job and work to buy himself a replacement car, his parents purchase him another one. This second one is not to Junior's liking, but it is all his parents can afford. Rather than thanking them for bailing him out of the trouble he brought on himself, Junior becomes angry with them for making him drive what he calls "an embarrassing little geek car." He does not let them forget his displeasure, and they feel badly that they could not afford one more to his liking.

Near the end of his senior year of high school Junior discovers that his girlfriend is pregnant. He does not feel ready to be a father, but she does not want to get an abortion. Junior blames her because she was not on the pill. He is greatly frustrated, because her irresponsibility will now ruin his life. To Junior's delight, she finally succumbs to his pressure and gets an abortion. He is relieved and vows to start taking advantage of the free condoms passed out by the school nurse.

Before going to the state university Junior enrolls in the local junior college. Midway through his first quarter, however, he realizes that his grades will be too low to get him into the university. His first twelve years of school had been too easy, and most of his teachers too accommodating—he never learned the importance of meeting deadlines and working hard for grades (his parents were always there to help him do his homework). He meets with each of his instructors to explain that "C"s are just too low for him—he insists they have to give him better grades. A couple of them agree to work with him, but the others refuse, explaining that grades must be earned by meeting the standard and completing assignments on time. Rather than own his

Appendices

responsibility, he feels quite the victim of inflexible, unfair teachers who are ruining his future.

Concerned for their son's future, Junior's parents visit the school administrators to complain about their son's unreasonable instructors. Despite pressure from his parents, the teachers are backed up by the administration, so Junior's parents take out a second mortgage on their home and enroll him in a private college in another city. It was not what he had planned, but Junior begrudgingly accepts his new school.

In his new college Junior buys prewritten term papers and occasionally cheats on tests as he makes his way to graduation. Like so many college students he studies some, but he parties and plays plenty, too. He has no addictions, but drinking, smoking marijuana, and sleeping with girls are a part of his college life. After four fun years he graduates and lands a job with a big corporation. Needless to say, he has a difficult time adjusting to inflexible work hours and bosses who will not tolerate "goofing off" during work hours. His water cooler conversations with fellow employees are often about their demanding and unreasonable managers.

Eventually, Junior falls in love with a gal, marries, and settles down to have a family of his own. Between the two of them they make good money, and feel they can afford to be generous, so they buy Girl Scout cookies and every December they make a small donation to help save the rainforests. They are saving up to buy a home, so decide to put off starting a family right away.

After three years Junior is laid off from his job, so he looks to his parents for financial help until he can find other employment. Having been dissatisfied with his last employer he is picky about his next job, so lives off his wife's income, unemployment compensation, and his parents' gifts for a year before accepting a new position. During his season of unemployment he also re-cultivates a friendship with an old girlfriend from college. By the time he starts work with his new employer, his wife files for divorce, explaining she has had enough of his "laziness" and his extramarital "friendship." Junior feels unfairly abandoned and quite the victim of unwarranted treatment. He tells his tale of rejection to anyone who will listen and wins the pity of most everyone he knows. He moves back in with his parents until he can recover from his grief.

Junior is a man who was raised to believe that his personal happiness was supreme. The will-to-be-gratified he had as a toddler was never brought under check by his parents and flourished throughout his childhood. In the formative years when he should have been learning self-restraint, he was allowed to grow in self-indulgence. He grew up with an over-exalted sense of his own importance and little tolerance for delays of pleasure. Because he was rarely required to take complete responsibility for himself, and because he was continually rescued from facing the consequences of his actions, he came to believe that everyone owed him. And because the same was true for most of his friends and classmates, he shared their belief that pursuit of personal pleasure without consequence was a supreme right. Looking back to his childhood we can see how he developed that outlook on life. True, he did not become a gangster or drug dealer, but he did arrive at adulthood with the same self-focused view he had as a toddler. This outlook on life affected his relationships with his wife, his employers, his community, and his parents. Is it any surprise that it also determined his approach to politics, and subsequent political associations?

Appendix B: The story of Sky

Sky is barely a toddler, but has few limits around his house. His parents think it is bad for a child to be excessively restricted or constrained. *"Too many boundaries squelch creativity,"* they would say. Yes, to keep him safe from harm, everything that might pose a threat they moved out of reach, but otherwise, Sky had complete freedom to wander anywhere he wanted and get into anything that piqued his interest.

One time Mom walked into the kitchen to find it covered in organic whole-wheat flour, and three-year-old Sky sat there in the middle of it, thoroughly pleased with his extreme kitchen makeover. She wasn't even tempted to anger, because she was delighted that he had "explored" and "discovered." She even sat down with him and threw a little flour in her hair, to show her support. For her the clean-up was worth the "freedom to express" that Sky was developing.

Mom and Dad had almost no rules in their house. In fact, it was their opinion that a child should be allowed to say whatever he wanted to say, and never be forced to do anything he didn't want to do. Gaining his cooperation was, therefore, a major effort—they had to talk him into everything. And as you can imagine, reasoning with a three-year-old is near impossible.

One day they discovered that this approach to parenting had its drawbacks. Shortly after boarding a plane for a family trip to Florida, they were kicked off the flight, because Sky refused to sit down and buckle his seat belt. Mom almost got into a fistfight with a flight attendant who had attempted to force Sky into his seat. It was at that point that Mom and Dad realized, until Sky was older and better able to understand issues of personal safety, they would take all their trips by car.

Sky's parents did not force him to do anything he didn't want to do, except in one area—they insisted that he eat healthy foods. Fortunately for them he developed his appetite for healthy food early on. From the time he was six months old he was given raw broccoli, jalapeno peppers, and green sprouts to nibble on, so—unlike his peers—Sky learned to loathe sweets and love vegetables.

When Sky was old enough to go to school his parents were concerned that his free spirit would be stifled by the structure of the classroom setting. Consequently, they chose to send him to a K-8 Montessori school with an extremely unstructured learning environment, which would allow him the maximum freedom to study the subjects that most appealed to him.

Little did they realize that because Sky was not learning to subject his will to adult authority and submit to boundaries and structure while young, he was growing up with an over-exalted sense of his own importance and would later have difficulty cooperating with rules and submitting to authority.

Sky's parents were holdovers from the '70s. They ate healthy, revered the environment, and smoked marijuana daily. Although they indulged Sky with the freedom to do whatever he wanted, he was not indulged with possessions. They lived a simple, non-materialistic life, and Sky was content with that.

While he was growing up, the evenings in Sky's home were not spent in front of the television. He learned from his parents to play the guitar and conga drums, so free time was spent with the family playing music, reading poetry, and discussing philosophy. Most discussions were about how to save the earth or improve humankind.

By the time Sky reached high school he was quite the individual. A total nonconformist, he dressed in mismatched clothes and rejected deodorant because he considered it a ploy of big business to manipulate sales.

Having been raised to "question authority," he was fearless in the articles he wrote for the school newspaper. He castigated not only his philosophical enemies, but his allies as well, if he thought they lacked consistency. To make his voice heard outside the school, he also submitted some of his articles to the local newspaper as letters to the editor. His outspoken ways kept him in constant conflict with teachers, because he could not receive instruction without arguing. He was quite impressed with himself and his ideas, and rejected the notion that he should do anything with which he didn't agree. Because he loved to debate, Sky joined the school debate team, but quit in the first month—there were too many rules for him.

By the time Sky got into college, his convictions about the environment and his upbringing to "stand for what you believe in" were compelling him toward all kinds of activism, and he regularly participated in protests and demonstrations, no matter what the cause. If he heard about pro-lifers who were gathered at an abortion clinic to protest the killing of children, he would help stage a counterprotest. Immediately following that, he might join with some likeminded friends to protect some trees threatened by loggers. Sky and the others would chain themselves together and surround a tree in hopes of slowing down the logging process. In his mind their efforts were not a protest—they were on a rescue mission—literally saving the life of a tree. Although he was arrested for his actions, and the trees were cut while he was being processed through the jail, he felt victorious because he had done what he believed was right.

The more Sky was arrested the more galvanized he became in his views and the more confident he grew in his view of his own goodness. He never ate meat or used any animal products, he didn't wear anything made from animal hide, and he rode his bicycle everywhere he could—even in the rain, unless the trip was too far— then he would catch a ride in a friend's car. He even limited his use of toilet paper, choosing instead to use squeeze bottles of water. Sky's willingness to live by his convictions and suffer arrest gave him a sense of superiority, and he condescended to most others— especially liberal leaders when they behaved hypocritically on environmental issues. He would fire off a letter to the editor when liberal celebrities would attend fundraisers for the environment and leave their limos outside idling, polluting the atmosphere and contributing to global warming. He would grow angry when he would read of environmental defenders who flew private jets to their events, and whose palatial mansions were massive generators of fluorocarbons.

It was when one of his environmental heroes was speaking at his college that Sky was first arrested in a solo protest. During the question and answer time Sky was given the microphone and allowed one question, but as you can imagine, Sky insisted on asking multiple questions and making many comments. Unwilling to relinquish the mic and cease his domination of the Q & A session, campus police were asked to physically restrain Sky. But because Sky lacked the ability to do that which seemed unreasonable to him, he was subjected to a Taser gun. Five separate discharges were required before he would comply with police instructions and stop struggling. He was carried outside and placed in a squad car, but was later released without charges once everyone had left the building. Since no one had ever forced him to do anything against his will previous to that night, he felt like the ultimate victim of injustice. He just could not comprehend the concept of submitting to an authority greater than himself, without arguing. His obligation to close his mouth and obey a police officer was, therefore, way beyond his ability to fathom—in his mind he had a right to discuss their instructions.

Sky had been raised to *care*, and he found himself angry with those who didn't. It was because he cared so much about others and the earth that he was intolerant of anyone who lacked his view of tolerance. He could not see the hypocrisy in tolerating only those views with which he agreed. This became especially evident one day during a peace march. While he and three hundred others were marching to protest the war overseas, a handful of counterprotestors were present in support of U.S. troops. The counterprotestors held signs that challenged peace protestors—they read, "Are you REALLY for peace? How are things at HOME?" This was too much for Sky—he lashed out with his peace sign and struck the nearest war supporter who, interestingly enough, didn't retaliate. What a picture for the evening news—peace activist lashes out in violence while war supporter restrains himself peacefully.

No, Sky could not see his own hypocrisy—resorting to violence in support of peace. But he also didn't understand the reason he was so offended by the challenge "How are things at HOME?" You see, Sky's relationship with his parents had always been great growing up—they had no rules, so he was never in rebellion. They shared the same values, liked the same music, and smoked the same marijuana. The generation gap that emerged in the '60s did not exist in his family. Things had been absolutely wonderful at home—until his first year of college. That was when things changed.

Sky's parents had been getting together regularly to have coffee with an old friend of theirs who had become a "Jesus freak." These meetings were scary for Sky because he noticed his parents changing. They had believed in Mother Earth and despised the idea of a Divine Being to whom we were accountable, but now they were reading the Bible. After several weeks they finally had time to sit down and explain to Sky that they had become Christians. Their announcement confirmed Sky's fears and sent him into a tailspin of anguish. Their lifestyle change and their new views were intolerable to him. Although they still liked to play music together, they no longer wanted to smoke weed with him, and in fact, asked him not to smoke it in the house. And although they never judged Sky for his values, he imagined they thought they were better than him. This change meant that their evening discussions were not the same—for in his growing-up years none of them believed in absolutes, so no one was ever "wrong," but now discussions would frequently break down in disagreement. However, it was Sky who was upset—not his parents—they were more at peace than ever.

The more Sky took offense at his parents' beliefs the unhappier he became. That day when he struck out at the counterprotestor, it was because he was stung when his hypocrisy was exposed. While a few of the other peace protestors felt ashamed when they realized that they marched for peace, but warred at home with their parents, Sky reacted in anger. He didn't want to face his own hypocrisy, so he attacked the one who made him feel guilty. And such was Sky's life—he stood against what he called intolerance and hatred, yet he himself was hateful and intolerant of all who offended him. One day he might see his hypocrisy, but not as long as he found security in the good feelings he had about himself.

Appendix C: The story of Devon

Devon was conceived as a result of a one-night stand. Abbie, his mother, was nineteen years old, single, and living off of welfare when he was born. He came into the world in a county-run hospital, and his formula, diapers, and baby food were purchased with food stamps.

Devon never knew his real father, but his mother had many live-in boyfriends over the years. Each time she got a new boyfriend it meant that Devon moved into a new house or trailer. Between boyfriends he and his mom would live in their car.

When Devon was eight years old, his mother moved in with Mark, who was different from all the others. Mark didn't ignore him—he seemed to want the father role in Devon's life. He gave him chores to do, forbade him from "sassing" his mother, and "walloped" him if he misbehaved. While Abbie was serving a six-month jail term for possession of illegal drugs Mark assumed the responsibility of parenting as much as he knew how. Of course, he didn't know much, because he was raised in a dysfunctional family himself.

Although Mark tried to be Devon's father he wasn't exactly a good role model for him. Mark, you see, was a small-time drug dealer. Devon learned from him how to lie, cheat, steal, and "work the system."

When Devon got into trouble at school, which was frequent, Mark or Abbie would go down and meet with the teacher. However, from their perspective, nothing was ever Devon's fault. To them Devon was only in trouble because the teacher didn't like him. Even when Devon was caught red-handed, they rejected his responsibility and accused the teacher of playing favorites and treating him more harshly than others who did similar things. Needless to say, Devon grew up prone to self-pity and with quite the victim mentality.

Smoking, drinking, and drugs were part of Devon's life. Neither Mark nor Abbie directly encouraged him in substance abuse, but because their own lifestyle modeled it, and these things were readily available, Devon partook whenever he wanted. By the time he was eleven years old he was smoking cigarettes every day.

Pornography was ever-present in Devon's home, and he had his first sexual encounter before he was twelve. It was with a neighbor girl whose innocence had been taken by her stepbrothers. Devon learned early on that women were to be used and abused.

When he was twelve years old Devon got caught burglarizing a neighbor's house. Since it was his first offense he was released into the custody of his parents. In response, Mark beat him—not for the crime, but for getting caught.

The beatings had never been unbearable for Devon—he learned early on to toughen up and not care when Mark beat him. What he hated, however, was being verbally shredded by his mother. His body could handle the blows, but his heart felt ripped apart every time she lit into him. She had no idea of the power she had in her son's life or the effect of her words. As time wore on, the more he was demeaned, the harder his heart grew.

By the time he was thirteen Devon convinced himself that he didn't care anymore.

It was about that time that Devon was drawn into a local gang. It offered him what he was missing at home—value, significance, and a sense of belonging. The gang members made him feel appreciated—they even nicknamed him "Razor," because he was already shaving.

"Razor's" membership in the gang meant that his crimes grew from simple burglaries to violent attacks and robberies. Mark didn't approve of Devon's gang association, because he didn't want the attention their crimes might draw back home. When it became apparent that no amount of intimidation was going to convince Devon to break ties with the gang, Mark and Abbie decided to relocate. They wanted to find a place where there were no gangs. One day while Devon was at school they gathered their meager belongings and loaded them into a trailer that Mark had stolen just for this occasion. As soon as Devon arrived home they got him into the car and headed off to a small town in the mountains.

As you can imagine, Devon was completely devastated. The gang that had given him a sense of identity—that had made him feel like somebody—was gone from his life. Now he was stuck out in the boondocks—in "hickville" as he called it. Devon knew how to stuff down his feelings, so he told himself he didn't care. He *did* care, but he just buried his misery and anger.

Devon's new home was a two-bedroom trailer that sat in the middle of ten acres of forest. It had lots of trees, but also plenty of poison oak, and Mark couldn't have been happier—he finally had a place where he could grow his own marijuana. They had lived off of welfare, disability, and food stamps, but Mark had always sold drugs as a supplemental income.

Within the first few days after moving in, Devon discovered that the town was full of trusting people—nobody locked up anything. And Devon's compulsion to steal was something Mark hadn't counted on. In a big city, when a crime is committed, there might be tens of thousands of suspects to consider, but when a new pattern of crime develops in a quiet little town, the first to be suspected are the town's newest members.

It wasn't long before the local sheriff paid his first visit to Mark's marijuana farm. Fortunately for Mark, his acre of young plants was well hidden behind poison oak and went unnoticed by their visitor. Devon however, was not so fortunate—he was sitting on a stolen bike when the sheriff pulled up.

Devon was able to convince the sheriff that he was not intending to keep the bike, but had planned to return it to its rightful owner all along. Mark assured the sheriff that he would deal with Devon and mete out an appropriate punishment; the sheriff trusted everyone's sincerity and left with the bike in his trunk.

Mark, having come too close to the law, had never been so angry with Devon and proceeded to attack him like never before. Devon, however, aware that he had grown almost as big as Mark, decided to stand his ground and fight back. They traded blows for a few minutes before Mark paused to nurse a cut lip. As he did, Devon ran out of the house and headed for town. In gym class he had always hated running, but with his adrenaline pumping he didn't stop running for the entire two-mile trip to the courthouse. There he found the sheriff and spilled the beans about Mark's acre of weed.

This was a life-changing day in Devon's life.

Mark was in jail before the day was over, and Devon's mother was angrier than she had ever been—she tore into him with her words. In a profanity-laced tirade, she cursed the day he was born and demeaned him by ridiculing his every weakness and flaw. She exposed his vulnerabilities and emasculated him like only an intimate acquaintance can do.

Devon hadn't cried in years, but he couldn't hold it in any longer—he burst into tears and ran from the house crying and screaming. He was hurt and angry—he hated his life and wanted to end it. The thought of jumping off a cliff ran through his mind, but he feared he would just injure himself and spend the rest of his life in a wheelchair. As he ran he devised a plan—he would hitchhike back into the city and move in with one of the guys from his old gang.

He did indeed catch a ride back to his old neighborhood, and was able to find a friend whose parents were willing to take him in, but it was only a week before Social Services got involved. They placed Devon in foster care—where he stayed until his eighteenth birthday. He never saw his mother again.

During the four years he was in the system Devon bounced from home to home—seven in all. He liked living in nice, clean houses in which the "parents" didn't scream or hit him, but he didn't like rules. He could speak respectfully to his foster parents if he had to, but when he was out of sight he did whatever he wanted. He stayed out late, snuck around at night, and cut school. He also took whatever he set his eyes on, even if it belonged to the foster families who cared for him.

Tragically, Devon never understood or appreciated the kindness he was being shown by those who took him in. He had lived on government handouts for so long he had developed the perspective that everything he received for free was owed to him. This point of view was so deeply woven into his thinking that when rebuked for his lack of gratefulness he was completely incapable of seeing it. In fact, such admonitions would only make him angry.

By the time Devon was twenty years old he had been in and out of jail several times. To his "benefit" he once had been stabbed in jail, which left him with a limp and allowed him to collect disability benefits. Between his disability income, his live-in girlfriend's social security, and the welfare benefits she received for her two children, he felt he didn't need to work a job.

Devon had never joined a political party and had never voted, but he knew which of the two major political parties he wanted in power. He and all his friends knew which party was more likely to take care of them and ensure that they could maintain their lifestyles.

Appendix D: The story of Reb

Reb was born in the early fifties, the second of four children. His father worked a blue-collar job and his mother stayed at home to raise the kids. His parents and grandparents on both sides were dyed-in-the-wool Democrats.

By the time Reb was two his parents decided he was old enough to start learning some self control; so like his older sister before him, and like most of the children in his neighborhood, Reb received a spanking each time he refused to obey his parents. The spanks were always delivered in a calm and restrained manner, and never in anger or out of control. Subsequently, neither Reb nor his siblings developed violent tendencies—to the contrary, they grew up self-controlled and respectful of authority.

Living off of one income, his family didn't have much extra money. This meant that neither Reb nor his siblings had lots of "stuff." They had necessities, but weren't indulged by any means. Time after time he watched his parents count out their loose change to decide if they could afford a purchase. Countless times he heard them cancel an errand because they wanted to save the gas. To say they lived frugally puts it mildly.

Reb, like his sisters and brother, had few expectations, and was appreciative for everything he was given. There were even times he refused a dime from his mother for ice cream, just to save them money.

Reb's parents had been raised in the Great Depression, and knew the meaning of hard work and responsibility. It was therefore something they wanted to pass on to their children. This meant that Reb had to do chores—daily and weekly. He never liked jobs like pulling weeds—in fact, he hated them—but it never crossed his parents' minds to exempt him from hard work, just because it was *hard*. In this way Reb was forced to learn the meaning of personal responsibility; faithfulness in duties earned privileges, and laziness, deceitfulness, and irresponsibility merited disciplinary consequences.

Reb's training at home paid off in life. He got above-average grades, never got into trouble at school, and kept the same after-school job for four years until he went away to college.

Although his parents were diligent in his training, Reb was a self-determining individual who had to decide what he would do with the lessons they had taught him. It was in his heart to be respectful toward adults and he generally tried to obey all rules, but he had his times of misbehavior. When he was young he would sometimes sneak off before he could be assigned a chore, other times he would read his sister's diary, and of course, he and his siblings had their share of squabbling. Not outrageous behavior in comparison to some, but he violated his conscience just the same.

By the time he was a senior in high school Reb had forsaken many of the morals his parents had sought to give him. He was still self-disciplined enough to exercise *some* moral self-restraint, but he started smoking marijuana occasionally, drinking at parties, and gratifying his prurient interests. Like so many teenage boys in that era he wanted to lose his virginity.

Within a few months of his senior year Reb had stopped smoking weed, because he didn't like the way it clouded his thinking. He continued to drink at parties, but two beers was his limit, and he refused all hard drugs. He lacked confidence with girls, so when graduation rolled around he was still a virgin.

In the summer after high school Reb was having the time of his life. He found a store that sold alcohol to minors, drove a racing Mini Cooper, and was having more success with girls than he had ever had. That summer, with a girl he hardly knew and cared very little about, Reb lost his virginity in a one-night stand. Things couldn't have been better.

(Here's the part of this scenario that some readers may be afraid to read, for the following is a brief, but straightforward discussion of "religion." Some are uncomfortable with such topics and don't like to be trapped into reading them, so this warning might help prepare you for what follows.)

Reb had grown up going to church with his family and was a strong believer in God. He believed in Him because he didn't have enough faith to believe that the universe could exist by chance. Everything from the design and power of the atom to cellular regeneration to the beauty of sex spoke to him of an intelligent and powerful designer. When Reb looked at humans he saw intelligence and personality—evidence to him that the Creator was more than an impersonal force. God, he was convinced, had personality and was therefore knowable.

Interestingly enough, Reb's belief in God didn't make him a religious person—just the opposite. Since Reb believed in God he knew he was answerable to Him and accountable to get to know

Him. But Reb loved running his own life too much, so chose to ignore that God existed. He was too self-consumed to be religious—a relationship with God just wasn't convenient. This was his thinking up until the summer after high school graduation.

It was just a few weeks after his "initiation into manhood" that Reb started dating Jade—a sweet and innocent girl that he liked very much. Little did he know that she would prove to be his undoing—in a good way.

One evening while sitting with Jade on the side of a mountain, Reb was trying to share with her a bottle of Boone's Farm Apple wine. After resisting his offers, she finally told him she wasn't interested because she was a Christian. Nothing could have distressed Reb more—he didn't want to date a Christian—he wanted somebody with whom he could "party." Making matters worse—she told Reb he needed to give his life to God. "Oh great," he thought, "now she's evangelizing me!"

Reb felt in his heart an obligation to give his life to the One who had made him, but he was so aware of his own moral failings that he didn't believe God would accept him, and he told Jade so. What he didn't know at the time was that awareness of one's moral failings opens the door to reconciliation with God—it doesn't close it.

Having grown up in church Reb had heard many times what Jade was trying to tell him. "Jesus died for your sins. They were already paid for," she insisted. "Jesus died only for sinners, Reb. He doesn't reject them when they come to him for forgiveness and a fresh start."

It all sounded too good to be true, but Reb had other things on his mind that night. Needless to say, he gave up on getting Jade drunk, and they left the mountain.

The next day Reb was still feeling the impact of his conversation with Jade. Reconciling with God didn't sound too impossible after all. Maybe there was hope for someone as rotten as Reb. He spent the day pondering—could God really love him enough to have someone else die in payment for his sins? Without realizing it, he was on the edge of a dramatic transformation.

It seemed too good to be true, but by the end of the day Reb found himself willing to believe it. And before he knew it, in just one day, his life had changed.

How does one describe a radical, spiritual conversion experience? It is not a person deciding to subscribe to a new creed, and then turning over a new leaf to change himself—it is not a self-generated experience at all. It is a person's mind suddenly becoming clear as a result of being touched by God. It is new life flooding into a lifeless soul, instantly changing who a person is. Reb had not attended a church service, recited a formula prayer, or participated in any religious rituals. He hadn't done anything but embrace the conviction that Jesus was the Son of God and had sacrificed His life to suffer the penalty for *Reb's* sins. That is all Reb had done, but he found himself suddenly transformed in his heart and his mind. He felt like a burden had been lifted off his shoulders and he was clean and new on the inside—none of which he knew to expect.

Hardly knowing what had happened to him, he realized he had lost his desire to get drunk and to sleep around. His values had suddenly changed and he sensed he had power to be different. He had gone through a radical metamorphosis in just one day—in minutes really—he felt like he had been *reborn*.

The next morning Reb woke up madly in love with God.

As Reb walked in his new life he couldn't believe the changes he was experiencing. It seemed to him like he had new eyes, and was stunned by how differently he saw life. He had once lived in fear of what others thought of him, but now he discovered that his insecurities no longer ruled him. For the first time in life he felt free to be different. He found himself bold to speak of Jesus to others, even though he knew many would react in anger and spurn him.

With a new outlook on life, Reb was determined to make a difference in the world, so he went to college for a degree that would allow him to help people in need. After graduation he found employment in the mental health field, but soon became frustrated with the lack of significant life change he saw in most psychiatric patients and the lack of long-term freedom he observed in substance abusers. Leaving that field, he took a job with a utility company while he went to seminary at nights. He decided that the best way to help people find deep and lasting change was to be a pastor.

In the midst of working and going to grad school Reb got married and started a family. When he had children of his own he found himself appreciating the principles of discipline, respect, and accountability he had gleaned from his parents. Not only were these things invaluable for the rearing of his own children, but they dovetailed with his understanding of human nature, which proved critical in his counseling and teaching when he did become a pastor.

After Reb's conversion, as he grew in understanding of personal responsibility, he concluded that he no longer identified with the "progressive" morals and overindulgent love of liberalism. By the time he was thirty, Reb had left the Democratic Party. Although he reregistered as a Republican, his loyalty lay chiefly with God and principles of moral conservatism.

Some will wonder why I have included this scenario since it is a stronger illustration of religious transformation than it is of parental influence. I include this story, because I know there are some readers who finished the book and are feeling inspired to change their lives and the destiny of their children. Yet, they lack the power to make the changes. For those who know they need more than they have within them, I wanted to encourage them to place their faith in Christ and call upon God. He has mercy on all who come to Him humbly.

NOTES

Preface

1. Reb Bradley, "'What's happened to America?' The ultimate answer," *WorldNetDaily*, June 01, 1999, http://www.worldnetdaily.com/news/article. asp?ARTICLE_ID=16149.

2. Reb Bradley, "When bad parenting turns into border policy," *WorldNetDaily*, May 23, 2006, http://www.worldnetdaily.com/index.php? pageId=36297.

Chapter One

1. Dr. Karl Menninger, as cited at http://www.quotesandsayings.com/teachers/.

2. Dana Littlefield, "School shooter won't go free: Spencer was 16 when she killed 2, wounded 9 in '79," *San Diego Union-Tribune*, September 28, 2005, http://www.signonsandiego.com/news/metro/20050928-9999-7m28spencer.html.

3. *Indianapolis Star*, "School violence around the world," October 2, 2006, http://www2.indystar.com/library/factfiles/crime/school_violence/school_shooting s.html. Also referenced at http://www.nationmaster.com/encyclopedia/School-massacre%23Infamous-school-massacre.

4. Ibid.

5. WNBC News, "Previous Shooting Rampages in America," December 05, 2007, http://www.wnbc.com/news/14784274/detail.html.

6. Meg Sommerfield, "Classes to Resume at California School Where Gunman Killed 4 and Wounded 9," *Education Week*, published online May 13, 1992, http://www.edweek.org/ew/articles/1992/05/13/34olive.h11.html.

7. *Education Week*, "3 Killed in 2 Shootings in L.A., Ky. Schools," published online January 27, 1993, http://www.edweek.org/ew/articles/1993/01/27/18ky.h12.html.

8. CNN, "Columbine Report," April 20, 1999, http://www.cnn.com/SPECIALS/2000/columbine.cd/frameset.exclude.html.

9. Christina Hauser and Anahad O'Connor, "Virginia Tech Shooting Leaves 33 Dead," *New York Times*, April 16, 2007, http://www.nytimes.com/

2007/04/16/us/16cnd-shooting.html.

10. Disaster Center, *United States: Uniform Crime Report—State Statistics from 1960 - 2007*, http://www.disastercenter.com/crime/uscrime.htm.

11. Center for Disease Control, National Center for Health Statistics, *National Vital Statistics Reports* 57, no. 5, http://www.cdc.gov/nchs/data/nvsr/nvsr57/nvsr57_05.htm#table2.

12. Ed Rubenstein, "They never learn—educational test scores decline," *National Review*, October 28, 1988, http://findarticles.com/p/articles/mi_m1282/is_/ai_6745946. Score of 980 converted to 1081 using the Recentered Scale.

13. U.S. Department of Education, National Center for Education Statistics, *Table 135: SAT Score Averages of College-Bound Seniors, by Sex: 1966-1967 through 2006-2007*, http://nces.ed.gov/programs/digest/d07/tables/dt07_135.asp. Scores based on the Recentered Scale.

14. Ann Landers, *Ann Landers Talks to Teenagers about Sex* (Fawcett Crest, 1963), 21-31.

15. J.C. Abma, G.M. Martinez, W.D. Mosher, and B.S. Dawson, "Teenagers in the United States: Sexual Activity, Contraceptive Use, and Childbearing, 2002," National Center for Health Statistics, Vital Health Stat., 23(24), 2004, 9, http://www.cdc.gov/nchs/data/series/sr_23/sr23_024.pdf.

16. According to a federal study released by the U.S. Centers for Disease Control and Prevention, one out of every four teenage girls is infected with an STD. Department of Health and Human Services, Centers for Disease Control and Prevention, "Nationally Representative CDC Study Finds 1 in 4 Teenage Girls Has a Sexually Transmitted Disease," March 11, 2008, http://www.cdc.gov/stdconference/2008/media/release-11march2008.htm.

17. AIDS infections have increased from 339 new cases diagnosed in the year 1981 to approximately 38,000 new cases diagnosed in 2006. In that twenty-five-year period there were almost a million new cases diagnosed and more than a half million AIDS-related deaths. Avert, "United States AIDS Cases and Deaths by Year," http://www.avert.org/usastaty.htm.

18. Have you ever wondered why so many "democratic" governments have risen and subsequently fallen in the last fifty years? With help from American officials, these governments are often patterned after our own, replete with a constitution, open elections, and limited federal control. It is not unusual, however, that these new governments eventually collapse or succumb to dictatorships, the reason being that a freedom-based approach can only succeed when individual citizens have the capacity to restrain or govern themselves. The more that individuals are ruled by passion, whether

it is anger, pride, covetousness, or lust, the more that government control is required to keep order. The more governments increase control, the more people feel oppressed and the more rebellion is fostered, and so on. Societal chaos is inevitable until citizens can rule their own fleshly drives.

19. Thomas Jefferson to Edward Everett, 27 March 1824, in *The Writings of Thomas Jefferson*, eds. Andrew Lipscomb and Albert Bergh (Washington, D.C.: Thomas Jefferson Memorial Association, 1903-1904), 16:22.

Chapter Two

1. George Washington to the Marquis de Lafayette, 7 February 1788, in *The Writings of George Washington*, ed. John C. Fitzpatrick (Washington, D.C.: Published by the George Washington Bicentennial Committee by authority of Congress, United States Government Printing Office, 1939), 29:410.

2. Arthur Brooks, "The Political Fertility Gap," ABC News, August 23, 2006, http://abcnews.go.com/GMA/Politics/story?id=2344929&page=1.

3. 2004 General Social Survey, as cited in Vicki Haddock, "Republicans' Fertile Future," *San Francisco Chronicle*, September 17, 2006, www.sfgate.com/cgi-bin/article.cgi?f=/c/a/2006/09/17/INGEJL45D11.DTL.

4. *Declaration of Independence*, final paragraph.

5. Samuel Adams to John Adams, 4 October 1790, cited in *America's God and Country Encyclopedia of Quotations*, ed. William J. Federer (Coppell, TX: Fame Publishing, 1994), 23-24.

6. James Madison, 1778, attributed in *Liberty! Cry Liberty*, ed. Harold K. Lane (Boston: Lamb and Lamb Tractarian Society, 1939), 32-33; unconfirmed.

7. Benjamin Franklin to the Abbes Chalut and Arnaud, 17 April 1787, in *The Writings of Benjamin Franklin*, ed. Jared Sparks (Boston: Tappan, Whittemore and Mason, 1840), 10:297.

8. Richard Henry Lee to Colonel Mortin Pickett, 5 March 1786, in *The Letters of Richard Henry Lee*, ed. James Curtis Ballagh (New York: The MacMillan Company, 1914), 2:411.

9. Benjamin Rush, *Essays, Literary, Moral and Philosophical* (Philadelphia: Thomas and William Bradford, 1806), 8.

10. George Washington to the Marquis de Lafayette, 7 February 1788, in *The Writings of George Washington*, ed. John C. Fitzpatrick (Washington, D.C.: Published by the George Washington Bicentennial Committee by authority of Congress, United States Government Printing Office, 1939), 29:410.

11. Cited in William V. Wells, *The Life and Public Service of Samuel Adams* (Boston: Little, Brown, & Co., 1865), 1:22, quoting from a political essay by Samuel Adams published in *The Public Advertiser*, 1749.

12. Thomas Jefferson to Peter Carr, 19 August 1785, in *The Writings of Thomas Jefferson*, ed. Albert Bergh (Washington, D.C.: Thomas Jefferson Memorial Association, 1903), 5:82-83.

13. Fisher Ames, *An Oration on the Sublime Virtues of General George Washington* (Boston: Young & Minns, 1800), 23.

14. Charles Carroll to James McHenry, 4 November 1800, in *The Life and Correspondence of James McHenry*, ed. Bernard C. Steiner (Cleveland: The Burrows Brothers, 1907), 475.

15. October 11, 1798, cited in *The Works of John Adams*, ed. Charles Francis Adams, (Boston: Little, Brown, and Co. 1856), 9:229.

16. John Adams to Zabdiel Adams, 21 June 1776, in *The Works of John Adams*, ed. Charles Francis Adams (Boston: Little, Brown, 1854), 9:401.

17. George Washington, "Address of George Washington, President of the United States… Preparatory to His Declination" (Baltimore: George and Henry S. Keatinge), 22-23. In his farewell address to the United States in 1796.

18. *Demoralized:* corrupted in morals; Noah Webster's 1828 *American Dictionary*.

19. *Depraved:* corrupt; wicked; destitute of holiness or good principles; Noah Webster's 1828 *American Dictionary*.

20. *Ab incunabulis* — Latin: from infancy.

21. *Irremissible:* to be punished and not ignored.

22. *Inculcation:* the action of impressing by repeated admonitions; Noah Webster's 1828 *American Dictionary*.

23. Thomas Jefferson to John Adams, 10 December 1819, in *The Writings of Thomas Jefferson*, eds. Andrew Lipscomb and Albert Bergh (Washington, D.C.: Thomas Jefferson Memorial Association, 1903-1904), 15:234.

24. Joseph Daniel Unwin, "Sexual Regulations and Cultural Behavior," address given on March 27, 1935, to the medical section of the British Psychological Society, printed by Oxford University Press (London, England). Library of Congress No. HQ12.U52.

Chapter Three

1. Terry G. Shaw, Ph.D., ABPN, "When Teens Struggle in School," Neurocognitive and Behavioral Diagnostic Associates, http://www.nbdaok.com/

articles/1.htm.

2. "Minnesota Crime Commission Report," *Journal of the American Institute of Criminal Law and Criminology* 18, no. 1 (May 1927).

3. *Married With Children,* FOX Network.

4. Ralph Nader, speech at Harvard Law School, February 26, 1972, cited at http://www.youthrights.org/quotes.php.

5. For most of world history the average minimum age for marriage in the majority of cultures (including America) was twelve for women and fourteen for men. It began to change in the U.S. near the turn of the twentieth century.

6. From a study in the book of Proverbs, Old Testament, Holy Bible.

Chapter Four

1. Ed Shipman (founder of Happy Hill Farm Academy/Home), from an interview published in the *Omega Financial Group Newsletter,* Winter 2006, www.omegasecurities.com/new_winter2006.htm.

2. Reb Bradley, *Child Training Tips: What I Wish I Knew When my Children Were Young* (Family Ministries Publishing, 2005).

3. *Look Magazine,* March 5, 1957.

4. The military understands well this principle and weaves it into the fabric of boot camp.

5. Even if we can afford gardeners and maids.

6. For help with understanding appropriate discipline, see *Child Training Tips.*

7. Some people think that teaching children to respect all adults makes them vulnerable to child molesters. With some children it definitely can. That's why we must also teach them there are times to respectfully say NO to adults.

8. For more help on how to cultivate love with your adolescent children, refer to my CD set *Influencing Children's Hearts.*

9. Both are available at www.familyministries.com.

Chapter Five

1. Churchill's version of a common platitude. Variations are ascribed to Mark Twain, George Bernard Shaw, Aristide Briand, François Guisot, Benjamin Disraeli, Georges Clemenceau, among others.

2. Ronald Reagan, "A Time for Choosing," speech broadcast as part of a television special *Rendezvous with Destiny,* October 27, 1964, transcript available at http://www.americanrhetoric.com/speeches/ronaldreaganatimeforchoosing.htm.

Chapter Six

1. Benjamin Franklin to the Abbes Chalut and Arnaud, 17 April 1787, in *The Writings of Benjamin Franklin*, ed. Jared Sparks (Boston: Tappan, Whittemore, and Mason, 1840), 10:297.

2. The most widely known of these studies was the Pygmalion Experiment, conducted by Robert Rosenthal at Harvard University in 1968.

3. Consider the duel between Vice President Aaron Burr and former Secretary of the Treasury Alexander Hamilton on July 11, 1804.

4. Gilbert Parker, *A Friend of the Commune*; Sid Fleischman, *By the Great Horn Spoon*; William Swinton, *Swinton's Third Reader*; Joe Baker, *Flowers for the Altar*, or *Play and Earnest*, etc.

5. *Memphis Commercial Appeal*, December 1, 1895.

6. Thomas Jefferson to Peter Carr, 19 August 1785, in *The Writings of Thomas Jefferson*, ed. Albert Bergh (Washington, D.C.: Thomas Jefferson Memorial Association, 1903), 5:82-83. Emphasis added.

Chapter Seven

1. Ann Landers, *Ann Landers Says Truth is Stranger* (Upper Saddle River, New Jersey: Prentice Hall, Inc., 1968).

2. Arthur Brooks, *Who Really Cares* (New York: Basic Books, 2006), 21.

3. Gary A. Tobin, Alex C. Karp, and Aryeh K. Weinberg, *American Mega-Giving: A Comparison to Global Disaster Relief*, Institute for Jewish & Community Research, 2005, http://www.jewishresearch.org/PDFs/MegaGiving_05.pdf.

4. Over the years I have offered odd jobs to many men holding signs, and have been taken up on my offers by only one. The transients I have known acknowledge that ninety-nine percent of those who offer to "work for food" are running a scam. They know that the message on their sign makes them appear responsible, and that most people would rather give them money than trust them in their home to work.

5. Obviously, human compassion dictates that in a medical emergency, care should be given even to an enemy, let alone to a lazy or irresponsible person.

6. According to results of the World Values Survey conducted by the University of Michigan, the top five nations rated for happiness are: Nigeria, Mexico, Venezuela, El Salvador, and Puerto Rico, none of which is known for

its affluence: http://thehappinessshow.com/HappiestCountries.htm, based on "Happiness in World Values Survey" 1995-2000.

7. Congressional Commission on Training and Gender-Related Issues, "Army Gender-Integrated Basic Training (GBIT), Summary of Relevant Findings and Recommendations: 1993-2000," May 2003, http://www.cmrlink.org/cmrnotes/gibtsp01.pdf.

8. Rowan Scarborough, "Military policing of sexes eats time," *Washington Times*, January 18, 2000.

9. Betty Friedan, "The Problem that has no Name," in *The Feminine Mystique* (New York: Dell Publishing Company, 1963), published on the Web at http://www.h-net.org/~hst203/documents/friedan1.htm.

10. Thomas Jefferson to Amos J. Cook, 1816, in *The Writings of Thomas Jefferson*, ed. Albert Bergh (Washington, D.C.: Thomas Jefferson Memorial Association, 1903), 14:405.

11. *WorldNetDaily*, "Poll: Republicans happier than Democrats," January 6, 2004, www.wnd.com/news/article.asp?ARTICLE_ID=36477.

12. *Gallup Health and Healthcare*, November 2007; http://www.gallup.com/poll/102943/Republicans-Report-Much-Better-Mental-Health-Than-Others.aspx.

13. ABC News, "*Primetime Live* Poll: More Republicans Satisfied With Sex Lives Than Democrats," October 18, 2004, http://abcnews.go.com/Primetime/News/story?id=180291.

14. Those who would like to stop and test their ability to identify parenting that produces liberalism can turn to Appendix B and read "The Story of Sky."

Chapter Eight

1. As cited in David Foster, *The Power to Prevail* (Nashville, TN: Warner Faith, 2003), 195-196.

2. Associated Press, "Private U.S. Aid for Tsunami Tops $200M," January 5, 2005.

3. *USA Today*, "Americans Give Record $295B to Charity," June 25, 2007, usatoday.com/news/nation/2007-06-25-charitable_N.htm.

4. Jo Knowsley, "Dyslexic sues bank—because he can't read his statements," *Daily Mail*, April 28, 2007, http://www.dailymail.co.uk/pages/live/articles/news/news.html?in_article_id=451419&in_page_id=1770&in_a_source=.

Notes

5. James Bone, "I only stole from horrible celebrities, says housemaid," *Times Online*, August 24, 2005, http://www.timesonline.co.uk/tol/news/world/us_and_americas/article558727.ece.

6. Associated Press, "Newspaper's reporters turned away from interview with governor," December 18, 2003, http://www.naplesnews.com/news/2003/dec/18/ndn_newspaper__039_s_reporters_turned_away_from_in/.

7. Charles J. Sykes, *A Nation of Victims: The Decay of the American Character* (New York: St. Martin's Press, 1992).

8. *Third Branch* Newsletter of the Federal Courts, vol. 39, no. 1, January 2007, http://www.uscourts.gov/ttb/200701/workload/index.html&qt=lawsuits+filed+in+2006&col=uscourts&n=1.

9. *USA Today*, "Judge: Web-surfing worker can't be fired," April 24, 2006, http://www.usatoday.com/news/nation/2006-04-24-websurfing_x.htm.

10. Associated Press, "A porn-surfing Michigan parole officer is getting his job back—with a raise, too," January 26, 2006, http://abclocal.go.com/wpvi/story?section=news/bizarre&id=3847601.

11. *WorldNetDaily*, "Tavis Smiley: Blacks too 'emotional' to obey rules," June 29, 2007, http://www.wnd.com/news/article.asp?ARTICLE_ID=56455.

12. NBC News 4 "Stealing For Salvation" http://www.youtube.com/watch?v=qygZC9ywc0Y.

13. *WorldNetDaily*, "Celine Dion: Let 'em loot!" September 04, 2005, http://www.wnd.com/news/article.asp?ARTICLE_ID=46143.

14. Associated Press, "Accused Shoplifter: Bowel Caused Crime," April 16, 2007, http://www.breitbart.com/article.php?id=D8OI05I80&show_article=1.

15. Caroline Davies, "Skunk-addicted schizophrenic fulfils sick fantasy by killing a black woman," *Telegraph*, April 03, 2007, http://www.telegraph.co.uk/news/main.jhtml?xml=/news/2007/04/03/nskunk03.xml.

16. BBC News, "Cue killer not guilty of murder," November 09, 2005, http://news.bbc.co.uk/1/hi/england/cornwall/4422446.stm.

17. *Local*, "Man gets sick benefits for heavy metal addiction," June 19, 2007, http://www.thelocal.se/7650/.

18. *WorldNetDaily*, CAPITAL letters in e-mails spark probe," May 27, 2007, http://www.wnd.com/news/article.asp?ARTICLE_ID=55897.

19. Joshua Rozenberg, "Judge bans husband from naming adulter," *Telegraph*, December 5, 2006, http://www.telegraph.co.uk/news/main.jhtmlxml=/news/2006/12/05/nban05.xml.

20. *WorldNetDaily*, "Judge gives child-rapist 60-day sentence," January 6, 2006, http://www.worldnetdaily.com/index.php?fa=PAGE.view&pageId=34215.

21. *Capitol Gazette*, "Molester gets 4 months jail: Prosecutors, neighbors blast light sentence," March 24, 2007, http://www.capitalonline.com/cgi-bin/read/2007/03_24-43/TOP.

22. *WorldNetDaily*, "'Slaps on wrist' for attacking Minutemen," March 29, 2007, http://www.wnd.com/news/article.asp?ARTICLE_ID=54926.

23. Alvin Powell, "Resolution sought in Mass. Hall standoff," *Harvard Gazette*, April 26, 2001, http://www.hno.harvard.edu/gazette/2001/04.26/01-sitin.html.

24. CBS News, "Teens' Near-Fatal Joke Roils Ohio Town," August 19, 2006, http://www.cbsnews.com/stories/2006/08/19/national/main1913829.shtml.

25. Tom O'Connor, Ph.D., "Emerging Defenses to Crime," accessed on Tom O'Connor's Austin Peay State University faculty Web site at http://www.apsu.edu/oconnort/3020/3020lect05a.htm, accessed September 29, 2008.

26. Those who would like to stop and test their ability to identify parenting that produces liberalism can turn to Appendix C and read "The Story of Devon."

Chapter Nine

1. Reb Bradley.

2. Nancy Gibbs, "Who's In Charge Here?" *Time Magazine*, August, 06, 2001, http://www.time.com/time/magazine/article/0,9171,1000465,00.html.

3. Associated Press, "Italian parents beat up principal over grades," March 3, 2007, http://www.msnbc.msn.com/id/10704040/.

4. For multiple examples of out-of-control parents, check out the Web site of National Association of Sports Officials and review their page of poor sports: http://www.naso.org/sportsmanship/badsports.html.

5. KCRA News, "Youth Football League Takes Action against Coach," September 5, 2006, http://www.kcra.com/news/9793508/detail.html.

6. Michelle Koiden, "'Cheerleader mom' freed after serving six months," AP News, March 1, 1997.

7. John Haney, "Knoxville father makes boy wear sign as punishment for using drugs," WATE News, April 18, 2007, http://www.wate.com/Global/story.asp?S=6390423.

8. Sarah Gordon, "Mom makes daughter who bullied hold a poster in front of schools," *Press-Enterprise*, May 17, 2007, http://www.pe.com/localnews/southwestarea/stories/PE_News_Local_D_bully17.3f7a9b4.html.

9. Christine Kraly, "Teen's now 'poster boy' for better conduct," *Northwest Indiana and Illinois Times*, February 23, 2006, http://www.thetimesonline.com/

articles/2006/02/23/news/top_news/d9766be05279c3ed8625711e0007bbd9.txt.

10. Associated Press, "'Meanest Mom on Planet' Sells Teen Son's Car After Finding Booze Under Seat," January 09, 2008, http://www.foxnews.com/story/0%2C2933%2C321239%2C00.html.

11. Kirk D. Richards, "Hit the showers, boys," June 17, 2005, *Columbus Dispatch*, http://www.dispatch.com/live/contentbe/dispatch/2005/06/17/20050617-D1-02.html.

12. Cited at http://thinkexist.com/quotation/we_now_know_a_thousand_ways_not_to_build_a_light/174628.html.

13. Charles Krauthammer, "Education: Doing Bad and Feeling Good," *Time Magazine*, February 05, 1990, http://www.time.com/time/magazine/article/0,9171,969312,00.html.

14. Ina V.S. Mullis, Michael O. Martin, Eugenio J. Gonzalez, and Steven J. Chrostowski, *TIMSS 2003 International Mathematics Report*, TIMSS & PIRLS International Study Center, Lynch School of Education, Boston College, http://isc.bc.edu/PDF/t03_download/t03intlmatrpt.pdf.

15. Center for Disease Control, "Trends in Reportable Sexually Transmitted Diseases in the United States, 2005," http://cdc.gov/std/stats05/trends2005.htm.

16. CBS News, *60 Minutes*, "The "Millennials" Are Coming," May 25, 2007, http://www.cbsnews.com/stories/2007/11/08/60minutes/main3475200.shtml. Story originally aired on November 11, 2007, and was updated on May 23, 2008.

17. Jeffrey Zaslow, "Blame It on Mr. Rogers: Why Young Adults Feel So Entitled," *Wall Street Journal* online, July 5, 2007, http://online.wsj.com/public/article/SB118358476840657463.html.

18. R.F. Baumeister, J.M. Boden, and L. Smart, "Relation of Threatened Egotism to Violence and Aggression: The Dark Side of High Self-Esteem," *Psychological Review* 103, no. 1 (February 1996) 5-33, http://www.apa.org/journals/rev.html.

19. Laura Clout, "Mary is contrary in the politically correct year," *Telegraph*, December 26, 2007, http://www.telegraph.co.uk/news/main.jhtml?xml=/news/2007/12/26/npc126.xml.

20. Ibid.

21. Tom Peterkin, "Police ban on marriage questions—for fear of hurting gays," *Telegraph*, http://www.telegraph.co.uk/news/main.jhtml?xml=/news/2004/01/19/npol19.xml.

22. Bob Unruh, "Now *Brits* ban 'mum' and 'dad,'" *WorldNetDaily*, February 1, 2008, http://www.wnd.com/news/article.asp?ARTICLE_ID=59990.

23. *Daily Mail*, "School bans Mother's Day cards," February 7, 2007, http://www.dailymail.co.uk/pages/live/articles/news/news.html?in_article_id=434754&in_page_id=1770.

24. Laura Clout, "Mary is contrary in the politically correct year," *Telegraph*, December 26, 2007, http://www.telegraph.co.uk/news/main.jhtml?xml=/news/2007/12/26/npc126.xml.

25. Casey McNerthney, "Booing at games may be banned," *Seattle Post Intelligencer*, March 3, 2007, http://seattlepi.nwsource.com/local/305898_booban03.html?source=mypi.

26. Laura Clout, "Mary is contrary in the politically correct year," *Telegraph*, December 26, 2007, http://www.telegraph.co.uk/news/main.jhtml?xml=/news/2007/12/26/npc126.xml.

27. *Metro*, "Football league bans reports" March 31, 2004, http://www.metro.co.uk/weird/article.html?in_article_id=5247&in_page_id=2.

28. *WorldNetDaily*, "Rules say homes must be safe for robbers," December 27, 2007, http://www.wnd.com/news/article.asp?ARTICLE_ID=59391.

29. Richard Savill, "Police won't chase if thief has no helmet," *Telegraph*, June 30, 2006, http://www.telegraph.co.uk/news/main.jhtml?xml=/news/2006/06/30/nhelmet30.xml.

30. Karen McVeigh, "Drug-addict inmates sue over 'cold turkey' detox," May 12, 2006, *Times Online*, http://www.timesonline.co.uk/article/0,,8122-2176806,00.html.

31. Ian Drury, "Brave Grandma Arrested after Standing Up to Yobs," *Daily Mail*, August 4, 2006, http://www.dailymail.co.uk/pages/live/articles/news/news.html?in_article_id=399145&in_page_id=1770.

32. Slander, defamation of character, yelling "FIRE" in a crowded theater when there is no fire, instigating a riot, etc.

Chapter Ten

1. A saying made popular by *The Shadow*, the 1937 radio crime drama series written by Edward Hale Bierstadt.

2. Much of this chapter was adapted from my *WorldNetDaily* commentary, "When bad parenting turns into border policy," *WorldNetDaily*, May 23, 2006, http://www.worldnetdaily.com/index.php?pageId=36297.

3. Associated Press, "Top EU official criticizes extension of U.S. barriers along border with Mexico," April 17, 2007; http://www.signonsandiego.com/news/mexico/20070417-2114-mexico-eu-borderwall.html.

Notes

4. *PBS NewsHour Extra*, "Civilian Militia Patrol U.S.-Mexico Border," April 6, 2005, http://www.pbs.org/newshour/extra/features/jan-june05/minuteman_4-06.html.

5. Associated Press, "Nearly 7 in 10 Mexican Migrants Enters U.S. Illegally, Says Mexico," December 19, 2007; http://www.foxnews.com/story/0%2C2933%2C317404%2C00.html.

6. Sam Quinones, "Mexico to give survival kits to border jumpers," *San Francisco Chronicle* Foreign Service, May 17, 2001, http://www.sfgate.com/cgi-bin/article.cgi?f=/c/a/2001/05/17/MN200449.DTL.

7. Giovannia Dell'orto, Associated Press, "14 Illegal Immigrants Die in Desert," *Washington Post*, May 24, 2001, http://www.washingtonpost.com/wp-srv/aponline/20010524/aponline090219_000.htm.

8. Steve Miller, "Families of 11 dead illegals to sue U.S.," *Washington Times*, May 11, 2002, page 1.

9. Associated Press, "Kin blame Border Patrol for couple's injuries," August 26, 2006, http://www.tucsoncitizen.com/daily/local/24051.php.

10. Associated Press, "Mexico Threatens Suits over Guard Patrols," May 16, 2006.